SPEAKING UP

SPEAKING UP
A Book for Every Woman
Who Wants to Speak Effectively

Janet Stone / Jane Bachner

Illustrations by Catherine Tvirbutas

McGraw-Hill Book Company

NEW YORK   ST. LOUIS   SAN FRANCISCO
MEXICO   TORONTO   DÜSSELDORF

Book design by Ingrid Beckman.

1 2 3 4 5 6 7 8 9 B P B P 7 8 3 2 1 0 9 8 7

Library of Congress Cataloging in Publication Data

Stone, Janet, date
Speaking up.
Bibliography: p.
1. Public speaking for women.   I. Bachner, Jane.
II. Title.
PN4193.W7S7   808.5'1'024042   77-7134
ISBN 0-07-061673-6

For
BETSY HOGAN

ACKNOWLEDGMENTS

The authors wish to thank Barbara Anthony, Frank Bachner, Jane Elioseff, Polly Grant, Alan Hewat, Susan Heyman, Joyce Johnson, Toby Klebenov, Artemis March, Linda Micheli, Alberta Richmond, Sheri Safran, Mary Lou Shields, Jene Stamps, Leigh Star, Viv Sutherland, Katherine Triantafillou, and Peggy Tsukahira.

Unlearning to not speak

Blizzards of paper
in slow motion
sift through her.
In nightmares she suddenly recalls
a class she signed up for
but forgot to attend.
Now it is too late.
Now it is time for finals:
losers will be shot.
Phrases of men who lectured her
drift and rustle in piles:
Why don't you speak up?
Why are you shouting?
You have the wrong answer,
wrong line, wrong face.
They tell her she is womb-man,
babymachine, mirror image, toy,
earth mother and penis-poor,
a dish of synthetic strawberry ice cream
rapidly melting.
She grunts to a halt.
She must learn again to speak
starting with I
starting with We
starting as the infant does
with her own true hunger
and pleasure
and rage.

MARGE PIERCY
To Be of Use

CONTENTS

INTRODUCTION

Dear Reader,

We each talk, with more or less success, all day long. How seriously we are taken, how often our point of view prevails, how well people get to know us, how far we advance in our work, and how successful we are in our personal relationships often depend upon our ability to express ourselves clearly and with ease and assurance. Unfortunately, women have been taught to form habits of word use, inflection, style—and, indeed, silence—that directly contradict the purpose of communication: exchanging ideas and sharing feelings. This book is about habits of speech that get in our way, undermine our confidence, reflect and perpetuate our second-class status and prevent us from getting what we need.

The information in *Speaking Up* focuses on examples from meetings, formal presentations, workshops and so forth, but it must be clear that every time you open your mouth you are making a speech. Except for muttering to yourself in the bathroom, all speaking is public speaking. When you argue with a delivery person, give instructions to babysitters, fire an employee, explain your feelings to a friend, answer questions in an interview or talk on the phone you are using your communications skills. If you aren't forceful and confident in those situations, a larger forum will only exaggerate your weaknesses. The diction, mannerisms, body language, voice and attitude that you use in private go with you into more public settings. So, the basic approach to more effective talking is to shape up every day speech habits. You can't "Y'know," "um...uh," gesture wildly or whisper your way through life and expect to be somehow different at a podium.

We hope *Speaking Up* will accomplish these three things:

- show you how to camouflage and eventually cure nervousness;

- evaporate the mystique surrounding "speechmaking" so you will understand it for exactly what it is—talking;

- help you to "clean up your act," become more confident and articulate all the time, not just for special occasions or audiences.

We think it is both especially important and especially hard for women to learn to speak well in public. In fact, we have been through the panic, the damp palms, the nausea and we *know* it's hard. It's hard because speaking is such a personal activity; one's personality and physical appearance are very much involved and on view. The stereotypes and myths about women that have affected us over the years have affected audiences, too, and stereotypes will determine to some extent how we are perceived and how our message is received.

If speaking up is so difficult, why should we learn to do it? First, because self-assertion is an important part of almost everything we want to do. Obviously politics, teaching, management, volunteer work, sales, the law and many other career/work choices demand poised self-expression. Second, being able to talk well makes life more fun. Finally, speaking out is a fundamental right of free people, one that was forbidden to women for many years and one we must not, we will not, lose again.

Although we have been leading workshops on communications skills for women since 1972, we have not yet found a book we could recommend to our students with much enthusiasm. Most texts make the assumption that it is somewhat bizarre to find a woman talking to a group in the first place; their antiwoman bias shows up in abundant "men only" examples. We hope that *Speaking Up* will be more practical than these textbooks (that don't mention sweating), more accessible than private coaching (that can cost as much as $4,000 per day), and more helpful with women's specific needs. Whether you are a novice who hopes to become adequate, or a good speaker who hopes to become excellent, this book is written for you.

Every woman is unique and valuable; your ideas, your experience and your understanding are important. We hope to help you polish and share that experience, because we believe it can only do all of us good to hear you.

Janet Stone   *Jane Bachner*

CHAPTER ONE

Out From Behind the Curtain

The World Anti-Slavery Convention held in London in 1840 was a turning point for American women. Some of the abolitionist groups who represented the United States were made up entirely of women, and, of course, their delegates to the convention were women. The male delegates objected strenuously to the women's participation, and after great debate voted to seat only men. Women were forced to sit behind a curtain just to hear the proceedings. They could not speak, they had no vote. These women had worked long and hard for the antislavery cause they so deeply believed in, and they had a great deal to say; to be denied a chance to say it was a bitter experience.

Two of the women behind that curtain became good friends and allies that summer. They were Lucretia Mott, a Quaker who had long been active in reform movements, and Elizabeth Cady Stanton, a much younger woman who at the time of the convention was in London on her honeymoon. They talked about the irony of their situation, they talked about the inequalities from which they suffered, and they talked about what they could do about it. On one occasion,

Elizabeth Cady Stanton went to hear her new friend give a speech in a local meeting house. She had never heard a woman speak in public, as indeed few people had, and Mrs. Stanton was thrilled. In the nineteenth century the right to freedom of speech was not customarily extended to women, and while it did not offend Victorian sensibilities for women to work quietly for good causes (behind a curtain), it was considered outrageous for a woman to speak in public...unwomanly, unladylike and unnatural. It was not coincidence that Lucretia Mott, like many of the early leaders of the women's rights movement, was a Quaker. The Society of Friends encouraged women to speak in meeting and even allowed them to be ordained. Mrs. Mott had been ordained a minister at twenty-eight and had spoken often.

Elizabeth Cady Stanton was impressed. Gradually she became aware of the overwhelming difficulty facing her and the other women working in the abolitionist cause; in order to be effective in freeing the slaves, both women would first have to free themselves from the restraints and strictures of Victorian femininity.

Eight years later at the first women's rights convention in Seneca Falls, New York, Mrs. Stanton made her own "maiden" speech, summing up what has moved a great many women since to begin speaking up:

> I should feel exceedingly diffident to appear before you at this time, having never before spoken in public, were I not nerved by a sense of right and duty...

Women have changed laws and customs since Mrs. Stanton's 1848 speech. We now speak everyday in public on a great variety of issues, for many causes and often just for fun. Those Victorian rules of womanly behavior that kept women quiet and frustrated in 1840 appear to have been discredited. Alas, the truth is that the underlying taboos haven't changed. Many of us are still uncomfortable (without being sure why) taking a stand, arguing a point or being in control of a group. We may avoid a promotion because the new job would demand much more public speaking, we may not ask a question at the PTA that needs to be asked because we would feel so uncomfortable standing up and challenging the speaker. Worst of all, we may just go along quietly in most situations because it "wouldn't be nice" to make noise about it or because we convince ourselves "it was only a minor point, anyway." A chilling example of this self-defeating conduct is the difficulty many women experience in self-defense classes trying to overcome their socialization enough to shout and holler when being attacked.

Unless we can speak up, persuade and convince, unless we have the power of speech, unless we have a say in what goes on, we are not in control of our lives. What are the ideas about femininity we have inherited that make it difficult for us to speak effectively?

If we were quickly to list the most important assets of a good speaker they would be a strong voice, good eye contact, erect posture, clarity and decisiveness, and self-confidence. None of these has ever been considered "feminine."

"Her voice was ever soft, gentle, and low; an excellent thing in woman." Many women grow up with that quotation; it serves as a standard. When we read the play *King Lear* we discover that when the line just quoted is spoken, Lear's daughter Cordelia is dead and Lear in his grief is saying that she may not really be dead, it was always hard to hear her.

As Dorothy Parker said when they told her Calvin Coolidge was dead: "How can they tell?"

And following the rules, women do not bellow, they do not shout, they do not declaim or orate, they do not or should not (according to conventional decorum) even speak much above a whisper. Women who have great clear loud voices are made to feel ashamed. Time and again at meetings of women someone will say with an embarrassed shrug, "I don't need a mike, my voice is so loud..." when in fact it is very hard to hear her from more than a few feet away. How often a lover or husband will say, "Don't you scream at me!" the moment a woman raises her voice even slightly. When someone who is opposed to the Women's Movement discusses it, he or she almost invariably mentions that it is "shrill"—a term also applied to "spinsters," very old women, and female politicians.

The truth is, if a woman can be heard at all (and especially if she is saying something the critic doesn't like), then for sure she's talking too loudly. "Harridan," "termagant," "scold," "fish wife," "shrill," "shrew," "nag," "magpie," "virago" ... the list of insults is long. It is interesting to note that many of these words also mean ugly, sexually foul, or old. There is no parallel male character anywhere in tradition; that is, a man the *sound* of whose voice annoys people. (The obvious exception is the stereotype of the male homosexual—and his behavior is clearly labeled "feminine.") The loud woman, in short, is still considered a sin against nature and most of us are so afraid of being typed as such that we go too far in the other direction. We are so fearful of seeming abrasive that we mumble and mutter and no one can hear a word we say. A good strong loud voice carries conviction and authority, and that is just exactly why girls and women are discouraged from having one.

A good speaker also establishes eye contact with her audience. She uses that eye contact to get feedback and to establish herself as open and straightforward. Although in some cultures, looking down is a sign of respect, white Anglo-Saxons usually interpret shifty eyes as dishonest and a direct gaze as sincere. Women are an exception to this rule. We aren't encouraged to look people directly in the eye; instead we are told to avert our eyes, not to stare; we are taught how to drop our gaze seductively and so forth. A woman who looks someone directly in the eye runs the risk of being thought aggressive, pushy or worse. Often an open direct gaze is considered a sexual invitation. According to this double standard, a "bold" look is not simply a courageous one. All of this is part of the dilemma system that women face every day. What is considered positive, admirable conduct in a man and in people in general is wrong and unnatural in a woman. To make matters worse, the standards by which people are believed, accepted, promoted and elected are the standards for men and for "people." A woman behaving as she was taught to behave, that is, acting "feminine," disqualifies herself as an authority and is rarely taken seriously.

Another traditional stricture on women that comes into conflict with good public speaking skills has to do with "women's place" and very literally our physical place. That place had been on the inside, behind closed doors. Women have not become public figures. Woman in the home, man on the street. It can be argued that this idea carries over into our work. Interior decorating is okay, architecture is not; selling from behind a counter or inside a shop is okay, but a traveling saleswoman is not; organizing or running a political campaign is okay, but being the candidate yourself is not. Clearly a woman on a stage or in front of a crowd is making a *public* spectacle of herself and that's "unfeminine." (Actresses were for many years held in the same contempt as harlots for this very reason.) A Pastoral Letter from the Council of Congregationalist Ministers of Massachusetts attacking the idea of women speaking in public when they first began to do so sums up rather nicely an opinion still around today:

> If the vine, whose strength and beauty is to lean on the trellis-work, and half conceal its cluster, thinks to assume the independence and the overshadowing nature of the elm, it will not only cease to bear fruit, but fall in shame and dishonor into the dust.

We have been discouraged by a lack of role-models—a view of other women in public situations. For many years, for instance, women worked as writers and editors for radio and television news programs but rarely appeared on air. We are challenging this exclusion, of course, but don't underestimate how difficult it makes public speaking for most of us.

Women are supposed to be beautiful, that's axiomatic. We get plenty of approval if we are gorgeous, sexy and well dressed. Unfortunately, the percentage of women who are beautiful (according to the conventions of the day) is about the same as the percentage of men who are beautiful—very small. Most of us have come to terms in our daily lives with not being "beautiful" and get along fairly well most of the time. We only become obsessed with how we look on rare occasions. The time you spend standing up in front of a group of strangers who are all looking you over is definitely one of those occasions. Making a speech can trigger every last one of your insecurities; it takes willpower not to hunch over and make screening movements with your hands. Strong self-confident posture is absolutely vital to any speaker, but very hard to achieve when we know that our skin "should" be softer, our hair shinier, our breasts bigger, our thighs smaller and our teeth sexier.

Although women today increasingly recognize how and why we have been conditioned to be obsessed with physical appearance, we can't change the brainwashing of a lifetime overnight. In all the stories, songs and pictures, the "pretty" girls still win happiness and the "ugly" girls still suffer. It is no wonder the nasty lurking fear that we will be thought unattractive is so powerful.

It doesn't help much to move from strictly physical appearance to the broader area of "charm." Here, too, we must struggle against daily reinforcement of traditional ideas of what is "charming" in a woman. Unfortunately, in many cases charm is equated with vague, indecisive lighthearted gaiety. A good speaker needs to be as precise and concrete as possible; the last thing any audience wants is rambling, giggly nonsense. Good public speech may be warm, but it must be strong, assertive and direct. (By the way, there are very different standards for charm for men and women. Women are expected to go on being charming in a youthful giddy way, while men's charm is encouraged to mellow and mature.)

Robin Lakoff* points out that "ladylike" speech prevents the expression of strong statements. (Language patterns such as rising inflections, and euphemistic expressions may stem from an attempt to avoid offending anyone.) We would say that excessively good manners are symptoms of being worried.

Anyone who takes on the responsibility of speaking her

* Robin Lakoff, *Language and Woman's Place*.

mind will encounter resistance. It is natural for people to argue, to resist being convinced, to insist that the speaker "prove it." That's what makes interesting question-and-answer periods and good conversation at dinner. Women, however, often run into a very special kind of resistance that is annoying and disruptive. This skepticism is based on an unconscious assumption that women can't know what they are talking about *because* they are women. Unless we confine our remarks to a very limited range of subjects we encounter grave doubts, open amusement, boredom or sometimes hostility. In fact, a woman is often ignored even when she does stick to "feminine" topics. (Perhaps you know the story about the woman in labor who says to her obstetrician, "I am in great pain...," and he says, "No, you're not....") The worst of it comes after you have spoken well, documented your evidence and finally proved your point. People will come up in utter amazement and say, "Wow, you really do know something about auto mechanics. How did a girl like you get interested in cars? Gosh, it's really something. Sam, doesn't she knock you out?" and so on until you want to strangle the whole lot of them.

Sometimes the general astonishment that you can talk gives way to real hostility. This may be caused by a genuine disagreement with your stand on the issues or it may be that your personality irritates someone, or (unfortunately) the "problem" might be your race, religion or national origin. This hostility may take the form of vocal open aggression (teasing, heckling, catcalling, boos, nasty personal questions) or be a more silent variety such as crossed arms or yawns. In any case, it is very unpleasant to have a bunch of people mad at you. It is, we suggest, especially upsetting to women. Study after study, with infants, children and grownups, has shown that women are taught to get what they want by pleasing people. Psychologists call this "affective behavior." (Pleasing men has been an economic necessity for many women; marriage has often been the only available job.) Because our self-esteem (not to mention survival) is so often based on what others think of us, we can be understandably reluctant to risk encountering disapproval. It isn't merely past brainwashing that silences us; it is knowing that "uppity" behavior may be punished.

When women are accused of being overemotional, the accusation sometimes means that women do not cope well with criticism or anger. There is some truth in that. It takes confidence and self-respect to listen to criticism objectively and decide whether it is just or not. If our self-image is based on positive responses from "critics," negative feedback becomes a trying emotional experience (especially since we are already fighting an internal censor who is saying, "You shouldn't have opened your mouth"). A good speaker cannot be afraid of disagreement, criticism or hostility. She must not have a chip on her shoulder and must be able to approach people singly or in groups with warmth and humor.

We want to help women to develop the kind of confidence that will allow you to say what you think anytime, anywhere. *You* must be the final judge of your performance. As Maya Angelou says: "If a woman allows other people's definitions of her achievements to encroach on her own understanding of her achievements it will wipe her out." We do not mean to imply that women have difficulties and do it wrong while men have no problems and do it right. There are, of course, many men who suffer torments when required to speak in public. Many, many male speakers are stupifyingly dull and could benefit enormously from the tips in this book. Furthermore, in our opinion, many female speech patterns and much female language is *better;* in no way do we consider male speech patterns to be "standard." In general, however, growing up as a boy is better preparation for becoming self-assertive than growing up as a girl. In our experience, the sources of stage fright for most women are similar.

Ironically, not only does a female speaker have to deal with hostility and her own fear of failure, she also has to learn to deal with success. Problems with success fall into two broad categories. The first is concern about power. Public speaking can be very powerful. A good speech can persuade, arouse, inflame and change the course of events. Because women are new to this kind of power, we don't take it for granted. We don't think it is our automatic right. We have fought long and hard to gain entry into the decision-making circles and we want to be correct, to do the right thing. This very fine sentiment often causes self-defeating behavior. We second-guess our decisions and present statements in an "I take it back" manner; we agonize over the consequences of our leadership. We have to stop using the language of the powerless, which means we have to start taking responsibility for what we say. It is silly to state, "Ten percent unemployment is completely unacceptable . . . don't you think?"

The second problem with success is fear that we will encounter the very great unhappiness predicted for successful women. This hostility toward strong women is often disguised as pity ("poor thing, I suppose she has to . . .") or ridicule. We grew up hearing about "career women" and how unhappy and unfulfilled they were. As Matina Horner's studies have shown, women have a motive to avoid success. We have been taught in a hundred subtle ways that successful women are unnatural and unhappy, that they lose the chance to be loved or to have children or to live happily ever after. We don't want this to happen to us. Of course, good common sense and a look around will show us that nobody lives happily ever after and powerful women are about as happy as anyone else. Unfortunately, our good common sense often fails us under the pressure of standing up in front of all those people.

"Femininity," like any other bad habit, can be unlearned. Speaking your mind is an integral part of participation in life as an adult. Those behavior patterns that make you less effective as a speaker and inhibit you all the time can be changed. It isn't simple, but it isn't impossible; it does take practice. Almost all of us are born speakers; we had to be carefully taught to sit down and shut up. Now is the time to unlearn that teaching.

CHAPTER TWO

Evaluating and Strengthening Your Speech Personality

It's not what you say,
it's how you say it.
AMERICAN CLICHÉ

A good speaker is like a good athlete: she makes it look easy. She has taken a hard look at herself and developed her skills in each of the categories that are fundamental to good speech: body language, words, voice quality, emotional tone and personal interaction with the audience. She is aware of the ways in which women characteristically undermine their strengths and defeat their purposes, and she struggles to avoid them.

But it *looks* easy; the audience is aware only of a smooth relaxed presentation. If you have been in that audience and thought, "Sure, it's easy for her ... but I couldn't do it," we're going to try to change your mind. We think you can do it and in this chapter we'll talk about how: what to look for, what to eliminate, what to change.

Women as a group have a way of talking that is as easy to identify as a Brooklyn accent. Most of us announce that we are both full of doubt and eager to please at any cost everytime we open our mouths. Even when that self-trivializing message is exactly the reverse of what we want to communicate, it comes out in habits of speech so engrained that we don't even notice them. It is ironic that speech, which can be our most potent ally in the struggle for change, can so easily defeat us.

There are hundreds of self-defeating speech habits. This chapter will touch on some of the major ones, to which your initial response may be, "I don't do *that*." Perhaps you don't. But just so you will be sure, we'll start by describing how you can find out exactly what you do: how you talk and how you sound.

There is only one perfect tool for analyzing your speaking habits: videotape. A film of you in action allows you to watch and listen as if you were your own audience. We use video-tape in our classes. But unless you have access to this expensive equipment through your school or business, you will have to be content with less.

Three other good ways of evaluating your speech habits are listening to tape recordings, watching yourself in a full-length mirror, and asking your friends to listen objectively and give you a critique.

Most of us are surprised (and disappointed) the first time we hear our voice on tape. The common response is "Oh, no, that can't be me..." You may hear fillers (um, er, uh), na-sality, high pitch, inane giggling, or any number of other horrors. But hearing yourself as others hear you is an important first step to a great improvement. Listen to yourself—others do.

Tape record a telephone conversation with a friend or record a family dinner hour. Make recordings of yourself reading, reciting speeches or telling jokes. Tape a fight with someone you love. Try to get a realistic sample of how you sound in as many situations as possible. A woman who says she's fine in conversation or in small groups and claims she only gets stuck when there is a big audience, probably isn't as fluent as she would like to believe she is in these small settings. The techniques for improvement we will suggest involve better daily habits, not magical schemes for pulling oneself together at the last minute for a big speech.

When you have a lot on tape sit down and listen to it carefully.

Next you want to find out how you look. Give a speech to yourself in a full-length mirror. It will feel extraordinarily odd but can reveal all that the tape recorder kept hidden: facial tics and grimaces, poor posture, spasmodic gestures, and so forth. A mirror is a poor woman's videotape machine.

If you ask a few friends what they like about the way you talk and/or the one or two things they would suggest you change, you may get an earful. "Well, aside from your mumbling ...," "It's the flapping arms that really drive me ..." Listen to what your friends say. You may not believe every word and you may discount one or two criticisms, but in general believe them.

Now, what are you going to listen and look for?

Body Language

Body language is the eloquent message we send with our stance and gestures. And when what we say with our body contradicts our words, people believe the gestures and expressions. Most body language interpretation is common sense. Slouch and you look tired and discouraged. Hang your head and refuse to face people and you appear embarrassed or ashamed. Clench your teeth or your fists and you communicate anger or fear. A list of the jumpy peculiar gestures people make out of sheer nervousness would be endless.

Some common distracting movements are foot tapping, finger drumming, lip biting, cuticle picking, nose wrinkling, head scratching and ring twisting. You appear less than sure of yourself brushing or tossing your hair out of your face, pushing your glasses up, pulling your clothes around and playing with something (a pencil, book, notes or whatever you've been able to carry to the podium).

Many women have adopted a completely self-effacing body language that might be called "the invisible woman." The message seems to be "Don't take me seriously, I don't take myself seriously. In fact, I am not even here." Those of us who are afflicted sit down in a way that won't offend the

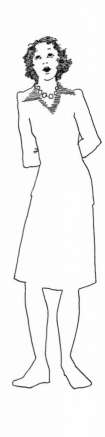

chair, continually walk around objects in our way rather than move them and have been known to say "Excuse me," when we walk into a wall. We try to adapt ourselves to the height of microphones. Rather than inconvenience the equipment by pulling it to mouth level, we end up looking like contortionists. Although it's a rare speaker who can sneak to the front of the room without awakening the audience, we have been known to try. We say "I'm sorry" in body language by talking with our hands clasped in front of us or talking with our arms behind our backs.

Women are often self-conscious about their bodies and uneasy about being objectified sexually. Those who have large breasts often refuse to stand up straight for fear of seeming brazen. In fact, most women have adopted one form or another of "ladylike" behavior. When we are self-effacing and ineffectual in the way we occupy space it is usually because we fear being thought "unfeminine."

The remedy for all this is exactly what your mother told you. Stand up straight, look people in the eye and quit fidgeting. Force yourself to let your arms hang loosely at your sides, force yourself to hold your head up (not cocked to the side) and just talk. It takes supreme self-confidence to just stand there. Quietly. It follows that if you can manage to just stand there, the audience will believe you are confident. You may even feel confident.

Eye Contact

The simple act of looking someone squarely in the eye is more persuasive than a hundred words. Eye contact in a speech does not mean simply scanning the audience and returning to your notes. Look at one person, hold her gaze until there is some response. Then turn to someone on the other side of the room, hold her gaze; then someone in the back. Eye contact is power. By looking someone directly in the eye you force a response, contact. It is interesting to note that pretending not to see or hear things has been a traditional "ladylike" way of dealing with unpleasantness. Some of us try to pretend the audience isn't there by staring over their heads or up at the ceiling or down at our notes. This makes the audience feel terrible.

Inappropriate Smiling, Joking and Laughs

It is our observation that some women smile constantly to cover an almost bottomless rage. Most of us smile inappropriately some of the time, particularly when we are angry or frightened but don't know what to do about it. We often smile at strangers, fellow employees, children, neighbors and so forth out of nervous habit. We would defend ourselves by saying we are just friendly, but in fact we are afraid *not* to smile.

This habit is self-defeating. If you make your argument while beaming at your opponent you neutralize it. When you know what you have to say isn't popular and put on a big apologetic smile you convey ambivalence, appeasement. You might as well keep quiet because a gesture of submission negates the force of words.

Far worse than the apologetic smile is the mirthless sound that punctuates many women's talk. It isn't really giggling or laughing although it sounds vaguely like it. It is an apology; an apology for speaking and an apology for existing.

We seem to be so afraid that we will be considered humorless or bad sports. Being a "good sport" is a one-down position in the first place. A good sport about what? As Evelyn Oppenheimer put it, "The oldest jokes in the world are about women and their constant chatter, their complacent disregard of facts and logic, and wives who talk their husbands to death."

An inordinate amount of what passes for humor is in fact strategic ridicule of women; new hat jokes, jealous of other women jokes, bad driver jokes and dumb blonde jokes are all considered "tasteful" enough for the daily paper, the *Reader's Digest* and good company. It is no mere coincidence that women who don't "get" or who are offended by jokes about vain, fuzzy-minded, extravagant, and imprecise women are often also spared the affliction of a convulsive, mosquitolike giggle.

Conversational Style

There are two ways of looking at male stereotypes about women talking. (Women nag, gossip, talk too much, talk about nothing, can't tell jokes properly, whine, are easily confused and don't finish what they started, and many others.) The first way is to deny them and point out that those kind of generalizations often reflect the misogyny of the accuser rather than the behavior of the accused. The second approach is to identify the nuances of powerlessness in our speech as a step toward eliminating them. The authors of this book think there is value in both approaches.

Contrary to popular opinion, women do not talk more than men. In our observation, men not only talk more often than do women, they talk at greater length and they interrupt other speakers more often than women do. Men usually talk almost to the exclusion of women at meetings and other "important" occasions. We would hate to see women adopt these argumentative, competitive styles.

Furthermore, we like a lot of things about how women talk. As a rule, women use more words, more interesting words, and use them better. We especially like the way women seem to encourage conversation by expressing appreciation, agreement and understanding. These are things we want to save. We want to eliminate ways we have been brought up to talk that broadcast confusion, powerlessness, insecurity, indecisiveness and a need for approval. (And we must become acutely aware of how our subordinate speech patterns are constantly reinforced by daily interaction in mixed sex groups. See Chapter Ten.)

Qualifying every statement is an attempt to avoid sounding harsh. It makes us appear as if we do not know our own mind. For example:

"I'd sort of like to explain . . ."

"It's kind of the way we do things around here . . ."

We also indicate insecurity by reinforcing statements with words like "just" and "really" as if we don't expect to be taken seriously unless we add the extra emphasis. If there is a description less clear than "interesting" it has to be "really interesting."

> "It was really raining hard . . ."
> "I'm really not in the mood . . ."
> "I really think we should go . . ."
> "It was just awful . . ."
> "I just don't know what to say . . ."

A surgeon who announced, "I really think you have a tumor and I'm just going to have to operate," would be frightening.

Women have been conned into believing that unmodified, unqualified statements are rude. In fact, most people find straightforward statements reassuring.

Avoid exaggerated superlatives in responses to ordinary situations:

"That is just divine . . . fantastic . . . marvelous . . ."

Overly dramatic speech is characteristic of insecure people with no real power. Although when theater people talk this way it can be very entertaining, it is impossible to imagine the President speaking flamboyantly for the very good reason that he would instantly lose his reputation for levelheadedness.

Robin Lakoff describes the habit of "tag questions" in *Language and Woman's Place.** A tag question is a mini-inquiry tacked onto a declaration. "The speaker is perfectly certain of the truth of her assertion, and there is no danger of offense, but the tag appears anyway as an apology for making an assertion at all." For example:

"It's hard to make speeches, isn't it?"
"We've been standing here a long time, haven't we?"

Of course, some tag questions are legitimate:

"I've got a cold. This one smells like blueberry, doesn't it?"

Rising inflection indicates a question: "Ready?" "Ready!" The way we know the first is a question is that the pitch of the speaker goes up when she says the word. The second "ready" is spoken with the pitch going down and is a statement. When someone uses rising inflection for statements that wouldn't ordinarily call for it, she indicates uncertainty. Women often do this unconsciously. We have built ". . . if it's all right with you . . ." into our whole personality.

"What time is your friend coming over?"
"3:00?"

* Robin Lakoff, page 14.

"What are you going to do today?"
"Oh, clean the house?"

This habit is particularly unsettling when the statement is unassailable:

"What is your name?"
"Janet Stone?"

It is our impression that women tend to hedge statements by ending them with "... wasn't that right?" or "... okay?" or "... don't you agree?" or "... right?"

Avoid self-effacing use of diminutives ("I have a few little ideas"), and try not to modify firm opinions with "I guess" or "I suppose."

Finally, if you are addicted to passive construction, you fail to take credit for what you have accomplished.

"When Jeanie was being born ..." instead of
"When I gave birth to Jeanie ..."

"Women were given the right to vote ..." instead of
"We won the right to vote ..."

This grammatical passivity may reflect the pressure we feel toward psychological passivity. Many women speak as if "I" were not in their vocabulary.

"This report was written ..."
"After the Committee was formed ..."
"When the garden was planted ..."

The fact that she wrote the report, formed the committee and planted the garden seems to have escaped the speaker's notice. Don't evade responsibility for your actions. Let your syntax reflect both your successes and failures. "I lost $1,000 in the stock market," "I initiated the suit ...," "I did it."

One final hint: try to stop saying "hopefully," "awfully," "got," "great," and "okay." "Hopefully" is the misplaced adverb of the decade. (Moreover, it can make the speaker seem to depend on fate rather than her own capabilities. "Hopefully, I will get up on time tomorrow." "Hopefully, I'll get in shape for the tournament.") The others are overused and can become verbal tics.

Confined Life Talk

The charge that women's subject matter is tedious is often simply a matter of narrow male standards of what is important or interesting—standards that the authors reject. It is commonplace to assume that women with young children talk of little else and are boring. Boring, we might ask, to whom? Students who are in their first year at Harvard Business School also talk of little else and are also boring—excruciatingly so, in fact—except (and here's the key) to other MBA candidates.

There are life and death situations (when your children are little or when they are teenagers; writing your Ph.D. thesis; psychoanalysis; internships; and having an operation) that are understandably absorbing to the one who's involved but may leave the rest of the world cold. Male society has decided that women are boring and what we do is trivial. It is important to notice that the women who decided to quit talking about floor polish and join the women's revolution are still accused of being shortsighted, smallminded and dull by the media. It isn't the content of their talk—it's something else. Gloria Steinem is a bore—is H. Rap Brown?

Any victim, male or female, of a highly routinized, low stimulus environment may degenerate by degrees into a vapid "How was your weekend?" conversationalist.

Does the subject matter of your daily conversation please *you?* If so, don't pay any attention when others label it "bureaucratic office chatter" or "unimportant small talk." If *you* are restless, stray out.

Voice

A strong pleasant voice is the greatest asset a speaker can have. Intelligence and wit are worth nothing if they cannot be heard. A high nasal pitch will destroy the most moving sentiment. Women like Barbara Walters and Shirley Chisholm, who have slight speech impediments, are considered good speakers but no speaker with a disagreeable voice quality can be considered good.

A strong voice comes in part from proper breathing. When we have students under our autocratic thumbs for eight weeks we can talk at length about breathing, demonstrate breathing and do slow exhalation exercises. However, to read about breathing is pretty insipid business. We're slipping in just enough information so that you can talk louder, project your feelings and overcome nervousness.

Good breath support comes from the diaphragm, which is the muscle you feel under your lungs when you pretend to blow up a balloon. If you allow your abdomen to slop out any which way you will not have enough volume because your diaphragm will be slack. Keep your tummy tucked in and stand up straight. Also keep your head up and shoulders down so that your chest is free to work.

Do *not* do deep breathing just before a speech. It does not relieve tension and you may pass out. Small sips of air, exhaled very slowly and regularly, work much better.

Hoarseness often comes on after you have been talking continually in a loud voice while feeling emotional stress or nervous tension. The throat tightens and this strains the vocal chords. Consciously relax your throat and depend on your diaphragm for volume. Clearing your throat repeatedly will only aggravate hoarseness.

If you sound like a giddy little girl, you will be treated like a little girl. A very high pitch says, "Don't expect too much of me. I am not a full-grown woman." Many of us have learned to use high-pitched kittenish sounds as an appeal that as much as says, don't hurt me. High pitch is the one vocal signature always associated with childish or immature speech.

Even those of us who normally talk in the lower range of our vocal register raise our pitch on emphasis words (adjectives, adverbs, words at the end of the sentence). Unfortu-

With this posture, these arms, it will be amazing if your friend can project her voice more than a couple of feet. Furthermore, she is sure to sound tired and depressed.

nately, this makes us sound frustrated, shrill and helpless. When your pitch goes down for emphasis you sound serious. Listen to yourself say angrily, "I hate you." A high pitch on *hate* will sound less convincing than a lower pitch.

It is not difficult to lower your pitch if you think it is too high. First, relax your throat muscles. Then, just for practice, groan a few times and say a few words in the lowest pitch you can manage. "Many brave men are asleep in the deep" is traditional, but you might like to try something else. How does it sound? Would you be able to talk that low in public without cracking up? If not, move up a bit higher and try again.

If you doubt the value of retraining your habits so you use a pitch that is somewhat lower, especially for emphasis words, sample these sentences in high pitch and then low:

"I *defy* you to produce the evidence."
"No, I *refuse* to accommodate that request."
"Children, it's *important* for me to get some rest."

The point is that pitch is purely affectation. It is true that the size of vocal chords varies and women and children generally speak in a higher pitch than men. However, the range any individual can speak in is enormous and mostly a matter of social expectation. A low pitch carries conviction and authority, which is why women are expected to whine.

Nasality

Talking through your nose makes everything you say sound complaining and disagreeable. A strident, nasal sound lacks chest resonance. It comes from general physical tension, especially in the jaw and tongue, which tenses and stays high in the mouth. When the jaw is clenched all sound comes up and twangs out the nose. Ugh. Regional accents often aggravate a nasal sound. The only sounds that should resonate in the head and throat are *m, n,* and *g.*

To correct nasality, open everything up. Yawn and feel how open throat muscles feel. Open your mouth *much wider* when you talk, and unclench your jaw. Now you should be able to feel a very slight vibration in your chest when you talk and none in your nose. Put one hand on your chest and the other on the bridge of your nose to make sure the vibration is right.

High whining nasal noises are frequently made by those (including children) who feel powerless and are trying to make a stronger person listen and pay some attention. (A more counterproductive approach is hard to imagine.) If you find that your pitch is high and you talk through your nose when you are almost hysterical with frustration and can't get anyone to care, then the remedy of course is not just speech exercises.

Self-limiting behavior does contribute to feelings of inferiority and to the impression of inferiority in those who observe you. However, you won't become powerful just because you lower your pitch or stop playing with your hair. The condition of women is more complicated than that. But you are bound to feel better if you sound stronger and that is a good start.

Volume

If nobody can hear you, you can't be held accountable for what you say. Low volume not only suggests low energy, low enthusiasm and weariness, it also suggests powerlessness.

Despite the myths about brassy women, we find that the most difficult job we have is helping our students stop murmuring and whispering. You must talk louder. We assume that right now you are saying either: I already have an incredibly loud voice, or: Oh, I couldn't. No you don't, and yes you can. The physical force it takes, the muscle control it takes to shout provides a psychological lift and makes you feel strong. It is no accident that yelling is an integral part of self-defense training. It makes sense. A little bitty soft weensy voice makes you feel little bitty soft and weensy. Remember, rabbits make almost no sound; neither do giraffes. The giraffe is not the king—or the queen—of the jungle.

While it is true that men dominate through interrupting or responding minimally to our remarks, we needn't collude in our exclusion. A woman who complains, "Nobody listens to me," or "I am never recognized in meetings," or "People interrupt me all the time," is often a whisperer. If the mutterer, mumbler and end-of-sentence–dropper thinks back, she may discover that the person who cuts her off in conversation today is a person who grew very weary of saying, "Speak up, I didn't hear you." "What?" "Huh?" Eventually people will stop trying to hear.

When you speak to a group, remember that the back row has just as much right to hear what you have to say as the first.

Warning. Volume comes from breath support in the abdomen and not from tight throat muscles. A taut neck with veins and cords standing out causes screeching. If you force your voice you will lose it.

In our experience the "strident" woman, although common in fiction, is very rare in fact.

Words

There is only one foolproof way to use the best words and that is to write the speech ahead of time and stick to your prepared text. This is what we recommend that you do in every case. But what about situations where you can't write out what you are going to say—an interview, for example, or just an ordinary conversation? Our advice about words cannot be followed to the letter, but serves as a general guideline. If we took the care we would have to take in order never to make these mistakes in impromptu situations we would sound like robots. But in general try to avoid the following:

Condescending or pedantic language. Instead of saying: "For those of you who don't know . . . ," or other remarks to that effect, define your terms clearly in the first place. A confident speaker does not deliberately talk over people's heads. She doesn't need to experience the exquisite thrill of patiently—oh, so patiently—explaining what her words mean to the ignoramuses. Showing off is a by-product of insecurity.

Remember that "always" and "never" are words that start arguments. Also, try to avoid "should," "ought," and other prescriptive words. Even if you clearly include yourself in the category of those who "should," you may still sound preachy.

Overly formal or "fancy" phrasing is also irritating to your listeners. (For example, "to retire for the night," "find some other mode of transportation," "partake of a slight repast" and so forth.) People often say things that sound ridiculous because they want to appear sophisticated or intelligent.

Yet "pretentious" for one person may be natural for another. The trick is to talk like you talk. If you went to Vassar or Wellesley and can't help sounding like it, go ahead. You won't endear yourself to anyone by affecting defective grammar or by borrowing "ain'ts" and "gonnas." Speak in simple direct language.

Poetic, sentimental language. If you suspect you have written purplish prose, rehearse it in front of other people to see if you can get through it without blushing or feeling awkward. If it doesn't embarrass you and your "audio editors" agree your language isn't too flowery, then you are probably safe.

Slang. Slang is a secret language for insiders. Unless you are an insider, you will get it wrong. It is also dangerous to dabble in technical jargon that you don't fully understand. No one will feel warmer toward you because you pretend to be like them. If you are, you are. If not, so what?

Acronyms and initials. Give things their full title the first time you say them (e.g., "the Women's Army Corps, or WAC's"; "equal employment opportunity, or EEO, for short"). You never know who will not understand what you mean.

Stereotypes. Beware of the word—or even the idea—"typical." There is no such thing as a typical foreigner, politician, preacher, conservative, Yankee, redhead, poet, farmer, Jew, housewife, longhair, reactionary.

Vagueness. Do not depend on inflection alone to provide meaning if there is a chance that you will be quoted. A sentence can read with quite a different meaning than it had when it was spoken. Irony, jesting, indignation are better written-in than inflected-in if the press is covering your talk.

Fillers. A filler is a word or phrase or noise used to fill space when you can't think of the right word or when you can't think at all. For example, "Uh...and uh...ummmm... ya'know...I mean..." The solution is to say *nothing.* Once again, we are dealing with a confidence problem. It takes poise simply to be quiet and think when you are having difficulty. Try to resist asking, "y'know?...y'know?" at the end of every sentence. Resist beginning sentences with, "Listen..." Other pads to avoid include, "Like...like...," "... an-da...an-da," and saying "I mean, I mean to say..."

Sexist language. Any word, phrase or style of talking that reinforces stereotypes about women is sexist. The philosophy behind individual cases may not always be clear. For example, what's wrong with the choice of "he" as the grammatically correct pronoun when the sex referred to isn't plain, as in "Every student should keep his notebook in his desk"? Or, why do feminists find it irritating that all references to God assume that God is male? If it isn't clear to you, we heartily recommend *Women and Words.** If the philosophy is fairly clear but you need examples and especially alternatives, McGraw-Hill's *Guidelines for Equal Treatment of the Sexes†* will spare you mistakes that could cost you credibility, rapport or votes.

Difficult words to say. If it is hard for you to say "penis" with equanimity, then you are better off avoiding it rather than blushing or dropping your voice. If you are embarrassed, your audience will be, too. However, there are no effective euphemisms for some situations, and it is far better to say, "He committed unspeakable atrocities," than to play down the truth ("Then he, uh, did, uh, you know, ah, he

---

* Casey Miller and Kate Swift, *Women and Words.*
† *Guidelines for Equal Treatment of the Sexes in McGraw-Hill Book Company Publications,* McGraw-Hill, 1221 Avenue of the Americas, New York, N.Y. 10020.

did it and then...," doesn't adequately describe sexual assault). Lastly, try to take into account the sensitivities of your audience. Just because you are comfortable saying it doesn't mean they can tolerate listening to it. Shock for shock's sake is adolescent.

Clichés. A cliché, which is an overused, overworked expression, became popular by being apt. It's a shame that "cold as ice," "heavy as lead," and "dry as dust" are hackneyed because they are expressive. If nobody had ever heard those comparisons before they would be perfect.

Diane White, a columnist for the *Boston Globe,* amassed a hilarious number of clichés for one of her columns. Here's a sample:

> burning issues
> coming down the pike or around the bend
> a matter of grave concern, sad state of affairs, crying shame
> fed up to here, same old song and dance
> seems like yesterday, a tear to the eye, once upon a time
> a hotbed of ____, a wasteland
> at that point in time, viable alternatives
> have to go a long way to top, cliché-wise, anything-wise
> state of decline, throes of death
> hard on the heels, in the same league with
> reached heights, in our life time, been going downhill
> bear the brunt of, enjoy a heyday, levelling criticism
> beating a dead horse, if you get my meaning
> out of the darkness, pave the way

Warning: there is an opposite extreme to being cliché-ridden. Don't try too hard to find dazzling metaphors and similes if what you end up with makes you sound silly. It is better to say "dead as a doornail" than "dead as a runover cat." In fact, it would be best of all simply to say "dead."

Variety, Pace and Emotional Tone

An interesting performance is based on variety. There are three basics that you can vary for effect: pace (how fast or slow you talk), pitch (how high or low), and volume (how loud or soft). If you feel strongly about what you are saying and allow your feelings to show, you will be an effective speaker. Your volume, tempo and pitch will vary naturally as you become involved with what you're saying. Unfortunately, fear and distance from the audience flatten out your personality. Unless you project yourself, you will appear static and lifeless.

Ask people you talk to everyday whether they consider you a fast talker or slow, a soft speaker or loud, and whether you have a high pitch or low. If the answer is "None of the above," great. You probably vary your pace, pitch and volume to suit the sense of what you are saying.

There is nothing more maddening than someone who talks too slowly. A fast, jazzy, frantic talker can make you nervous, but a slow one can make you homicidal. For some reason slow talkers seem to have a rather high regard for their own opinion. Thus, even though there is up to a two minute wait between phrases and it is hard to tell when they are through, they hate to be interrupted. We believe men suffer this affliction more often than women. It takes enormous arrogance to pontificate through hours of hideous exposition on one obscure point. However, if you think there is *any* possibility that you talk too slowly (people napping, people interrupting you a lot, glazed expressions), do us all a favor and speed up. Get out the old tape recorder and talk fast into it until you have improved.

If you talk too fast, it is sometimes helpful to concentrate on pausing between phrases and ideas rather than to try to slow down the actual rhythm of what you are saying. This gives your listeners a chance to catch up and "process" what you have said. When we discuss cue cards we will explain how to mark them to remind yourself to speed up or slow down.

Pitch. See earlier discussion of pitch. Remember, down for emphasis.

Volume. Once you get used to talking louder, then you have to learn how to talk louder and softer while, over all, you are talking louder. Nothing conveys emotions more effectively than a change in volume. We all have deep associations with loud and soft sounds that are easily triggered. Use them.

The only way you can improve the "drama" of your presentation is to take the risk of letting your feelings show. Showing your feelings slightly larger than life so they will project to the audience is hard. Experience is very important, but you do not have to get all of your experience in public.

Self-Evaluation

The student checklist on page 30 is the one we devised for our Speaking Up℠ classes.

Content Strengths
Use of humor
Easy to follow
Imaginative
Concrete examples
Visual language
Convincing docu-
    mentation
Persuasive detail

Content Detractors
Non-edited talk
Trivializing words
(sort of, little, etc.)
Cliches
Slang
Fillers
(y'know, like, um, uh)
Mispronunciation
Colorless vocabulary
Too formal
Misuse of words

Confidence/
Strengths
Calm recovery from
    mistakes
No apologies
Audible
Not too dependent
    on text
Relaxed manner
Willing to take
    risks/emotional,
    personal interaction
    with group
Strong posture
Warm smile
Direct eye contact
Animated face
Pleasant pitch
Good timing
Varied pace
Emphatic/meaningful
    gestures
Clear enunciation

Delivery Detractors

Too fast
Too slow
Sighing
Nervous smiling/
  laughing
Choppy pacing
Face:
  deadpan or severe
    look
  contortions (scowl-
    ing, mouthing)
  listless, apathetic
Hands:
  fidgeting/fussing
  waving around
  toying with _____
  tense, clenched,
    gripping _____
Eyes:
  rolling
  floor
  one side of room
  ceiling

contact with audi-
  ence not sustained
Voice:
  sing-song
  monotone
  nasal
  mumbling
  inaudible/
    whispering
  high pitch
  shrillness/stridency
  volume drops at end
    of sentences
  lacks variety in pace,
    volume
Body:
  tense, stiff
  shoulders hunched
  sloppy
  wiggling
Feet:
  shuffling, shifting
    weight
  crossed

Practice

Read poetry aloud. Rehearse inflection and variety of pace using letters and numbers à la "Sesame Street." Read other people's speeches—the more dramatic the better. If you have never encouraged your hammy side or if it has lain dormant since you played Mr. Tooth Decay in third grade, then speaking out will seem strange to you. Do it first alone and safely to give yourself a chance to get used to this new dramatic voice ringing in your ears. Learn the outside limits of your capacity to draw tears or cheers. "Performing" experience helps, even though you may never act like this behind a podium.

Getting Better

You are probably thinking that the whole thing is too much. And it would be too much to try to do all at once. The point is improvement. Strengthening your speech personality is a matter of establishing priorities. You can't fix everything all at once and in fact you can't fix everything, period. Begin at the beginning and go one at a time.

In our opinion, the basic, fundamental number-one items are as follows: stand up straight, look people right in the eye, talk loud, and be authentic. All the rest is gravy.

A word about being authentic. It means being willing to sacrifice "perfect" delivery for warmth. The reason we like and identify with some speakers and not with others has to do with believing one speaker. If you respect your audience and care about what you are saying and are willing to take the risk of exposing your real self, then you won't have any trouble establishing rapport—or recovering calmly from your errors.

It is common sense. It is probably what you have been telling yourself all along.

If your real issue is fear, read on.

CHAPTER THREE

Nerves

The "rules" that govern behavior are different for women and men. Too often, women's rules tell us to keep quiet, to hold back, to let someone else take the credit, to be diplomatic, to be sorry. These limits directly contradict what a speaker tries to do behind a podium. We spend a lot of time in our classes trying to pinpoint exactly what our students are afraid of, and over the years it has become clear that deep down inside they fear the penalties for breaking the rules of "appropriate" behavior. Only one student has ever said right out loud, "I want to make myself invisible"; many have acted as if being inconspicuous is an ideal.

It is very frightening to stand up in front of people who don't have to reveal whether they agree or not, and don't have to say whether they like you or not, if all your life you have sought immediate and constant reassurance. Most people don't like conflict (especially open conflict); many women have had to make "don't be mad at me" their motto.

Most of us have spent our lives trying to avoid situations where even the possibility of failure would arise. We put off testing ourselves and live on fantasies of what we will do, or might, or could do next month, next year, or if we felt like it. No wonder we are afraid. We don't have much realistic idea of our ability, of what failure feels like, or whether we can take the heat.

The following four handicaps (which we emphasize in treating student nervousness) are products of women's subordinate status in power relations in our culture.

1. *Lack of self-knowledge.* We have lacked opportunity to find out what we are good at. We don't even get to try on or fantasize roles. Self-awareness for women has been equated with "selfishness" and therefore has been taboo (except for awareness of personal appearance, especially negative awareness of pimples, pounds and gray hair). If one's range of options has been stunted from the early years, a career counselor's standard questionnaire about likes and dislikes, strengths and weaknesses, potential and under-utilized ability, etcetera, is almost useless. The answer to too many questions is "I don't know."

2. *Lack of practice.* It's hard to tell whether one is potentially capable of public speaking or whether it is fun to do if one's exposure is limited to two or three tries or even once a year.

3. *Lack of role models.* There have been so precious few women on the lecture circuit, in the boardrooms, on the six o'clock news, that it is hard to know what traits or styles it might be good to emulate. If you have seen very few women at the mike, then your "place" at the podium might automatically feel brazen and provoke your anxiety.

We ask students to name the female speakers they most identify with or admire, and to give their reasons. After lengthy silence, and some deliberation, there are lukewarm ballots cast for Barbara Jordan or Bella Abzug or a local television personality. Without lots of models to observe and learn from, women more or less teach themselves speaking skills. We assume the few women who are already public speakers had an even worse time.

4. *Lack of approval for trying.* Friends and colleagues react with incomprehension or total disbelief when the Speaking Up[SM] course starts to "take" (e.g., "Why, Sally, you've always been so quiet"). Our students report remarks like, "What do you want to do that for?" "What are you, some kind of show-off?" "That's getting pretty big for your britches, don't you think?"

When a woman begins speaking up for the first time she may hear, "Hey, you embarrassed me when you tried to talk at the meeting (dinner party, banker's office). I could have told them...," or "Boy, you were really something tonight; nobody could get a word in edgewise."

Your fledgling confidence can be undermined by friends. Perhaps they are frightened by this new you. They may say things to try to keep you from changing. If speaking your mind or assuming leadership tasks is met with disapproval, try to resist the rationalization that you didn't want to do it anyway.

What endears you to one group of people might estrange you from another. "Friends" who offer you acceptance on the basis of weaknesses are not helping you.

It is a psychological truism that a partner in a relationship all too often is not patiently suffering from the other partner's dependence or shortcoming; he or she is counting on it. For instance, if you and your friend are both on diets, do you team up to bolster each other's weakening resolves, or have you said, "This is too hard, *let's* hit the icebox."

This deadly togetherness, bonding for failure, perpetuates feelings of inadequacy. It is too easy to fall back on the feeling that your ambitions for yourself aren't really important, anyway. Reinforcement of low self-esteem in women is socially acceptable. Few object to the woman who doesn't speak up, who doesn't make speeches.

In fact, there is sometimes resentment when a woman refuses to collude with the "Let's don't try" offer of intimacy.

When you establish your friendship on the basis of support and mutual strengthening, rather than comfort of similar flight reaction to threat, difficult tasks become progressively easier. This is part of our strategy in forming classes on a peer group basis. Perhaps all the students are nervous, but they understand that a precondition of their registration is helping one another push on when it feels like quittin' time.

Then there is the equally devastating pseudosupport most common in marriages. That goes like this, "Gee, I'm really scared about the report I have to give tonight." "Then why don't you stay home?" Or, "You'll be fine, honey," without looking up from the newspaper. This sort of "helpfulness" is only an obstacle.

Those who may disapprove (usually in more subtle ways than the ones we have mentioned) are often the very people whose love you count on the most: parents, lover, best friend. The place to make your first speech may be to a friend or loved one who is hurting you by trying to hold you back. You may change the relationship to a supportive one simply by speaking up.

Women often say, "I'm all right if the audience is just women, but I really clutch if there are men." This fear is central to three major assertiveness struggles: a crippling need for male approval, an unrealistic dread of the outcome of assertiveness, and low self-esteem.

A woman who isn't nervous when there are "just" women may feel she doesn't count somehow and that the opinions of other women ("just the girls") don't count.

Of course, it is reasonable to be particularly nervous about the response of those who have power over you. Working women whose salary and promotions depend on a male boss's sponsorship suffer enormous conflicts about speaking up. Men frequently extend their approval to women who smile a lot, who rush to say a lot of nothing to camouflage the serious intent of an assertive statement, or who delight in being smart, "but not as smart as he is."

If we are ignored when we do well, we stop trying. If we

are ridiculed when we succeed at something "inappropriate" for women we feel different and out of place.

Yes, some of the outcomes of assertive action may be unpleasant. However, even if the result of your risk is one of the unfortunate possibilities we have outlined, remember that the alternative wasn't so hot, either. "Troublemaker" can be a nasty name for "pioneer"; "failure" can be a nasty name for "seasoning."

Solving the Problem

Only the speaker who doesn't care doesn't feel anything. Emotional reactions to an audience can be exciting, a buzz of anticipation, a slightly "up" feeling, a tingle. You are at your physical and mental best when you are keyed up. You don't do your best at a task you don't regard as sufficient challenge to cause a dither, a bit of fuming. If a seasoned performer loses her "good nerves" when she looks at a speech as a routine job, her relationship with the audience is jeopardized. We promise that if you speak in public often enough you will eventually know what it means to *miss* that toned-up feeling of intensity.

Unfortunately, the emotional reaction you have to an audience can also be panic.

There is a tremendous difference between the excitement that motivates an effort and stage fright, although the physical manifestations are similar or identical (e.g., perspiration, tremors). Genuine stage fright is so unpleasant that many of us sacrifice our careers or personal potential to avoid experiencing it.

Sometimes it feels like shell shock and your ears buzz. It is hard to remember the ordinary, to interpret feedback signals, to assimilate information. You feel "out of it." In this condition you have to take particular care to orient yourself, to ground yourself and to try not to do something strange. You're susceptible to such errors as talking too loudly or walking into a closet. Or fear may mean joyless laughter, breathing difficulty, foot jiggling, dry mouth, and other common symptoms.

No matter how frightened you are, it is important to remember that there is no real physical threat. The audience is just people. A speech is just talking. The novice will do well to allow a molehill to remain a molehill.

The Decision

We cannot guarantee you will completely lose your stage fright—there are always new audiences and new challenges that can trigger it. We can, however, offer suggestions to control stage fright, to turn it into a keen edge that will help you. Most students say that they are happier when they can hide the obvious signs of their fright so well that others don't detect them, even though the fear itself may remain.

Fear itself is not a good excuse. The mechanics of overcoming fear can be learned, and by going through the motions over and over again you can become strong. If you avoid situations where you have to use your brains and guts you'll reinforce cowardice.

Everyone begins as a beginner. The fact that others are "better" than you are is irrelevant. You, too, will be better the second time than you were the first.

You may notice that the people who do things are not necessarily the ones with the most ability. Those who "make it" are the ones who decide to use what ability they have and the ones who conquered fear. You can be your own heroine by deciding to do the same.

Psychologists call our advice "reaction formation." Musically, it's the "whenever I feel afraid, I hold my head erect and whistle a happy tune so no one will suspect I'm afraid" strategy.

We call it being brave and faking it.

If there were a magic formula to release a flow of brilliant, clear and fitting language for each occasion, especially the difficult early ones, we would reveal it to you. The fact is we all learn by doing. Maybe it will be easy and your improvement will be rapid. Or you may adapt slowly, through failure and error.

A hundred years ago people likely to end up in responsible positions (upper-class men) went through extensive public speaking training. Nowadays, most of us have to get "on the job" training.

In short, if your attitude is that you can't possibly do it, you'll never give yourself a chance. You have to speak in order to learn to speak well. There are no shortcuts.

I'm Afraid I'll Make a Mistake

The question is not how to avoid mistakes or nervous symptoms completely, because you can't; unfortunate things do happen. The question is how to plan so that you will make fewer mistakes and so that when you do make them you survive.

Great stars plan "mistakes." They think human frailty renders them more accessible to the audience and they're right. Of course, that's poor comfort to the rest of us who would rather be a little less human at this stage. But you can learn something from the idea of planning mistakes. It is easy to take a planned pratfall with charm and humor. If you aren't ready to plan your mistakes, at least you can decide what to do about the mistakes you are likely to make. Worry is the opposite of planning.

We take a strict problem-solving approach to nerves in our classes. Students are asked to think specifically about the errors or nervous symptoms they fear, and then devise a strategy to deal with them. The embarrassments haunting your imagination do happen to people. You cannot prevent everything. But you can recover.

One good way to counter a phobia is to give it its due. The things we fear are not silly if they stop us from trying. Here is the key: an audience will overlook or forget almost any horror if you allow them to. Poise, control, and a recovery plan can carry you through to triumph. Later, only you, your speech teacher and your mother will remember that your presentation wasn't perfect.

Throughout this section we will be giving you answers to the question "What if ... ?" All the answers have something in common. It doesn't matter what happens. What matters is your attitude toward what happens. That attitude should be unapologetic, good-humored, self-accepting and cool. How? By planning. Your secret fear may be original, but we bet it isn't. There are only so many ghastly possibilities. Some common fears are:

> Not being able to start speaking, standing there mute
> Having the audience laugh at you
> Losing train of thought, going blank
> Voice shaking and cracking
> Hands shaking, knees knocking, legs trembling
> Diarrhea
> Vomiting
> Sweating floods
> Fainting
> Boring the audience to sleep
> Tripping, falling down, walking into walls, dropping notes
> Crying
> Blushing
> Stomach rumbling, belching, farting, wetting your pants
> False teeth coming loose, glasses getting broken, wig falling off
> Saying some horrible faux pas, babbling incoherently
> Mispronouncing words
> Coprolalia (uncontrollable outburst of obscenity)

We won't address every anxiety on the list (and maybe your secret nightmare isn't even on it). The fundamental strategy remains the same in *every* case. You're standing there "with your face hanging out," as they say in television, with a choice. You can pull yourself together or you can come unstuck, compound your error, draw more agonizing attention to your difficulty and to your feelings of humiliation. Depending on what you do, the audience will either refocus quickly on your ideas or be forced to fixate on your disaster. Retaining the appearance of calm is half the secret to recovering calm. "Retaining the appearance of calm" means that you stop at one mistake. Instead of recovering according to a plan, we tend to let symptoms pile up in sequence until we feel overpowered by them (e.g., first the burp, which leads to wiggling and pawing the ground with your feet and to rising pitch, and so on). Stop at one. Relax, stay cool and forget it.

Getting Sick

If your stomach tends to go wild under stress, you can assume the speech will generate more than enough stress to upset it. Be prepared. If you get diarrhea, don't eat ahead of time and take a prescribed amount of an over-the-counter antidiarrhea medicine. If vomiting is likely, ask your doctor to prescribe an antinausea drug and arrange to have a trash can off stage (no, we're not kidding).

Although nausea can usually be controlled through slow exhalation breathing, it is comforting to have an emergency plan. When you arrive at the site of your talk, find out where the nearest bathroom is and figure out the fastest route to it. If you get sick in mid-speech, remember the audience will act like an audience—passive, willing to accept whatever expectations you set up for them provided you seem to know what you are doing. Excuse yourself with aplomb, say you will be right back, smile and make a dash for it. If you don't act like it's a big deal, they will just sit there and wait for you to come back.

We are describing guerrilla warfare on the part of your backward body. The body is a tool of the subconscious; it still believes that making speeches isn't nice. Think of your body as a sweet but old-fashioned relative. It will come around eventually if you are firm.

If you are on live television the moves are exactly the same.

When you make a mistake, don't telegraph it.

"I have to leave the set now, Barbara; I'll be back later in the show to answer a few more questions." Smile, exit, run. The host of the show is a trained professional; she or he knows what to do next and if she can't roll with the punches and ad lib, that isn't your problem. When Sally Quinn was doing the "Good Morning America" program she worried about having an "accident." A colleague told her about Walter Cronkite's professionalism carrying him gamely through an on-air attack of diarrhea. It wasn't a true story, but it could have been.

The Shakes

One thing you can do to practically guarantee trembling is to go all rigid with fear and refuse to move in any direction.

We recommend that you get out there on those watery legs and stride around. Release your grip on the podium, move your arms, use your muscles. If you lock your body in a single pose, your shaking can only grow more vigorous.

We think shaking is wonderful because although it is painfully obvious to the speaker, it cannot be detected by the audience. Time and again in our classes a student will confess that she thought her body would flat fly apart from trembling during her speech and her audience will be amazed and disbelieving. She looked fine to them. The shakes are disruptive only if you allow them to distract you; they are inconspicuous to others.

Remember to use cue cards rather than paper (which rattles in fear-palsied hands), avoid noisy bracelets and wear safe shoes (when legs turn to jelly, spike heels or wedgies are a menace).

A shaking voice demands more sophisticated planning because this symptom is noticeable. First, get rid of all the distracting apologetic gestures you've developed to go with the voice. (For most of us these are conspicuous swallowing, grimacing and head shaking.) Continue to make strong eye contact. Next, lower your pitch, pull in your stomach and increase your volume slightly. Do not inhale more air than you need to say your next phrase or sentence. If you do, you will wind up sighing out the excess or choking it back. A huge gulp of air escapes when you speak, causing you to sound squeaking, reedy and quavering. Too much inhaled air is also the cause of the panting and the jerky cadences that accompany a wobbly voice.

Tense facial muscles may tremble, too. Again, the symptom disconcerts the speaker but is seldom observed by the audience. Before going "on," hide in a private place and make faces. Blow up your cheeks. This is what television people do to relax a taut, rigid expression. If your facial twitches prevent you from smiling naturally, don't smile. Look interested instead. You can convey welcome and pleasure without baring your teeth.

Blushing

It takes grit to stand there blushing yourself into cardiac arrest. It isn't easy to ignore the accompanying pulsing sensations and pretend you don't feel like a bonfire. However, if you concentrate on your remarks and resist the impulse to complement the blush with other adolescent moves like shrugging or rolling your eyes, you will not only have overcome your problem but you will look better than the rest of us. Distances have a way of wiping out detail. Lights make most people look sick. A nice healthy blush will help compensate for lights and make you look terrific to row three and beyond.

Hot Flashes

A woman who is going through a difficult menopause and knows she may be subject to a hot flash should bring along several strong cotton handkerchiefs. Trying to mop a good hot flash with a "tissue" is silly. You're left holding a ratty-looking damp little wad. Handkerchiefs are better. The same thing goes for crying, by the way. Many of us have been made to feel ashamed of crying the same way we've been made to feel ashamed of menstruating or ceasing to menstruate or being hugely pregnant or other "crimes." Phooey. We are women. Sometimes we stifle crying, sometimes not. That's that. Take a handkerchief if you are likely to cry and get on with it.

Going Blank

When speaking impromptu or using an outline, it is common for a speaker to forget a word she wants to use. Stop and visualize what you are trying to describe if it's concrete; the word may pop out as soon as the picture forms in your head. If the word doesn't materialize, go ahead cheerfully with your talk. "...It's ah, ah...you know, ah...I don't know why I can't think of it, it's right on the tip of my tongue, damn, what is that word anyway...?" and so forth is just excruciating.

Remember that our concept of time gets a little warped in front of a crowd. If you have been winging it successfully up to the point where you go blank, remember that it only takes a moment or two of interruption to find your place in your notes; the pause is far better than babbling.

You may go blank about your whole subject, although this happens mostly in our nightmares, rarely in reality. (In fact, considering what we do say sometimes under stress, we often wish we had gone blank.) Like throwing up, going blank is your subconscious mind's revenge. You go blank because you don't want to say whatever it is that you had planned to say. Maybe you are afraid the audience won't like it, or your mother won't like it, or who knows what. Always carry some notes, however minimal, so that you can't cop out that way. Take your notes to the podium with you even if you don't think you will use them. The time you go blank may be the hundredth time you deliver the speech. We stress preparation and adequate notes precisely because it eliminates one more excuse. "Losing the train of thought" is an unnecessary worry. If worse comes to worst, you can just read your notes out loud. Nobody will be impressed with your skill as a speaker but you will have delivered your message and that's the whole point.

If you have absolutely no time to prepare and go completely blank, smile and say, "I have gone completely blank."

Saying the Wrong Thing—Bloopers

(From a statement by Lieutenant General Patrick F. Cassidy in the Fort Riley, Kansas, *Post*, as quoted in the New Yorker.)

I express to all the men and women of Fifth Army my heartiest congratulations. For the first time since 1947 our Army is free of the draft. We are moving rapidly as a professional force. The Active Army, Army National Guard and Army Reserve are now molded together as a team engaged in the struggle for the prevention of peace.

When you make a funny mistake, people laugh. It is not derisive or mocking laughter, but simple human enjoyment of something amusing. We usually say the wrong thing right smack in the middle of the most sensitive part of the speech. That makes it hard for us to join in the laughter, but join in if you can. Don't try to start again until you are sure the merriment has thoroughly died down.

What if you mispronounce a word, say words in the wrong order, begin to deliver card six before you have delivered card five, or inadvertently say the word that means the opposite of what you intend to say? The usual procedure is to make the correction and move on. For example: "The dorbal of the farm... The *or-deal* of the farm worker..." Don't bother to apologize, just stop and start over, eyes up, using strong emphasis and inflection to make the correction. Skip the correction altogether if you're pretty sure the word will be clear from the context. Radio and TV announcers slur words frequently but just sail right along.

If you totally screw up your script, make nonsense of a sentence, or take your ideas out of order and render them incomprehensible, you will have to explain. The audience deserves to know that *they* haven't suddenly lost touch with reality; it's you. Don't apologize ("I'm doing this poorly"); just do it again more clearly: "I'm going to go over that again—it wasn't clear."

When you repeat something correctly, do it eyes up. We have all seen a speaker reread a section of a speech she has blown, head nodding over the text, shoulders hunched over, nose practically in her notes. "Yep," she seems to be saying, "that's what it says all right." This makes her look dumb; she did write the speech after all.

Boring People

You begin a presentation aflame with enthusiasm, ready to be carried out on the shoulders of the crowd amid shouts of thunderous approval. Five minutes into the speech and you'll settle for no booing. As comedienne Joan Rivers would say, you're playing to "tired air." This happens to *EVERYONE*.

Performers say things like, "You're a great audience," because there are rotten terrible sleepy audiences who wouldn't wake up if you stood on your head. When members of the audience yawn, read their programs, gaze out the window or get up and walk out, it is very upsetting.

The worst thing you can do is to fall into a monotone muttering delivery as a way of pretending you're not there.

A bored audience calls for more risk taking, not less. Find two or three responsive, sympathetic faces and look to them for reinforcement. Play to them until your voice, your posture, your overall manner is jacked up. Care about them, communicate with them and use their positive feedback. If you can't find two sympathetic faces just do it for yourself. Since they don't seem to care anyway, think of it as a dress rehearsal and really work on polishing your performance. *What have you got to lose?*

Try to avoid getting strained and desperate. If it is hopeless and nothing you try seems to help, cut short the formal part of your presentation and move to questions and answers. Sometimes apathy is disguised hostility and things liven up when you give the audience a chance to explain why they hate you. If there aren't even any questions, then just stop. A dead horse is a dead horse. We repeat, this happens to everyone at one time or another, and although it is unnerving, we survive.

If you informed three or four people with your presentation but left the rest cold, it was not a failure. It is enough to be able to say with pride that you connected with a few of those who heard you talk. It's not that easy to persuade people.

Even if you are a great speaker who is having a "hot" day, with a dynamite talk, you will still miss about 20 percent of your audience. Some of the faces in front of you are unreachable. They are contemplating their impending divorces, or worrying about flatulence, and nothing will tempt them to listen.

Inelegance

What do you do about burping, coughing, sneezing, runny nose and itching? Say, "Excuse me," cover your mouth, blow and scratch, in that order. Do it vigorously, get it over with. You call unnecessary attention to these distractions by trying to be subtle with them. Nothing is more aggravating than little throat clearings and teensy sniffles that go on and on and never do the job.

Throat clearing is most often a nervous gesture, a habit, a stall. If you have a sinus condition, you probably already have a prescription for a nasal spray or decongestant. Avoid milk, beer, ice cream and grape juice on the day of the presentation.

And, obviously, you can't trust carbonated beverages.

Sweat

We know an ex-homecoming queen who defied the South Carolina heat by spraying deodorant all over her face before an "important" dance, but we do not recommend this technique. We do recommend large cotton handkerchiefs used with no apology. Mousy, surreptitious dabbing only makes you appear self-conscious.

Underarms can be taken care of by a trip to the dime store where dress shields still sell for under a dollar.

Dry Mouth

Fear causes dry mouth. So does a lot of talking and smiling —even your teeth can dry off. (To keep your smile from sticking at the gumline, rub a thin smear of Vaseline across your teeth.) A dry mouth sometimes makes a peculiar smacking sound, which can be distracting, especially if you are on a mike. Some speakers stick some sharp-flavored cinnamon candy under their tongues. You can always abrade your tongue against your teeth to make saliva flow. Ask for water at the podium and drink it when you need to. If your body is so rigid that pouring and drinking water makes you feel spastic, you aren't moving around naturally enough in the first place.

Major Klutziness

What if you trip, fall, drop your cue cards, knock the lectern off the table or walk into the flip chart? By now you must know the answer. The worse the mistake, the more important it is to maintain composure. If you want the audience to forget it happened you must carry on without fuss. It is your *job* to spare the audience discomfort by not betraying your own.

If a heel breaks as you cross the stage, remove both shoes and advance to the podium. If your glasses are knocked off the podium and shatter, you say, "I cannot deliver my prepared speech without glasses because I can't see, so let me tell you about Hope Houses..." Cope!

Of course, your first reaction is simply to lie down and die. Unfortunately, no matter how long you lie there, you won't die. You must go on, and you owe the audience something. They didn't come to see you fall down, after all, and while it was momentarily amusing they still want to hear you talk. Talk! Later, after you get home, you can obsess, agonize, hate yourself, cry and bore your family and friends to death.

Apology

Never apologize to someone unless you have injured her. Do not yell "Whoops!" or say "Oy, I just can't get it together today," or "Gee, I sure am a mess here." Do not smack your forehead in dismay, shake your head, rattle your papers, shift from foot to foot, squirm or wave your hands in agitation. What is the point of apologizing, verbally or non-verbally, for your shortcomings? To whom are you apologizing? No one is hurt because you forgot a word, mixed up your cards, broke into a sweat and tripped over a chair on your way out. Certainly, no one is injured if you were good, but not as brilliant as you hoped and expected. It is very hard to stop saying "excuse me, I'm sorry, forgive me, please, I beg your pardon..." We're sorry to be fat, sorry to be thin, sorry to be mothers, sorry to be Republicans, sorry to be gay, communists, antivivisectionists and gardeners. We're sorry we're so clumsy, and thirty-five, and conventional, and different, and talk too much, and not enough, and sorry we can't disappear altogether. If you don't believe it, just stop apologizing for one day. Forbid yourself even so much as a self-deprecating shrug. You'll see how hard it is.

There is silence after you make a statement and let it stand. There is silence after you forget your next word. Most of us can't bear that silence. And we fill it up with apology. Learn how to live with that silence and you will have learned almost everything you need to know about self-confidence.

How to Relax

Adequate preparation and good breathing techniques usually take the edge off all but the most vicious cases of nervous

She is not smiling at something funny. She is saying, "Please like me, I'm harmless."

tension. We also want to recommend a few tranquilizing exercises.

Offstage relaxers. The time finally arrives when there is, as you sigh to yourself, "Nothing left I can do except relax and go ahead with it." If you are offstage, in a radio studio, in the interviewer's anteroom or otherwise out of sight, sneak in a series of yoga neck rolls. You may either stand or sit to do them.

Shut your eyes and allow your head to droop forward as far as it will go, making double chins. While your head dangles, loosen your check muscles and let you mouth go slack.

Inhale, raise your head by turning it as far as possible to the right, hold for five seconds, exhale and return to the original hanging position.

Inhale, turn your head as far as possible to the left, hold for five seconds, exhale, and return to the original hanging position.

Inhale, and on one breath, slowly rotate your head all the way around, allowing it to hang down in front, to the right, in back and to the left. Repeat, rotating in the reverse direction. You may hear a "gritty" sound. Continue the exercise slowly until you feel your nervousness melt. This is an especially good tension reliever after prolonged desk work, too.

Another hint: From a standing position, bend over from the waist to allow your head and arms to dangle loosely toward the floor. Waggle your fingers. Slowly sway as though to sweep the floor with your hands from time to time. Remember to keep your neck relaxed by letting your head drop completely.

P.S. Know yourself—if you are not in shape, don't just flop over suddenly. You may never straighten up again. Those of us with bum spines have to approach this sort of thing gingerly.

Onstage relaxers. Check your hands for stage fright. Many of us clench our fists, wring our hands nervously (especially if they are cold from fear) or get white knuckles from grasping the podium or the arm of a chair. To calm yourself, allow your hands to fold into a limp but graceful pose in your lap, or if you are standing, allow them to hang loosely at your sides. It's very difficult to keep your hands limp and loose when you are nervous, but more important, it's hard to remain tense if your hands are relaxed.

Generally, keep moving but don't wiggle. A deliberate change of position from time to time will keep your circulation going, prevent your hands and feet from turning lavender and cold and make you feel more "normal." Wiggling, on the other hand, makes you feel childish and look worse. If you must cross one leg over the other, don't swing it. Avoid twirling your ankles in circles.

Diverting tension. Suppressed finger tapping or nail biting will seek some other outlet. We recommend that you find an inconspicuous way to let your body express tension as a stopgap measure until you no longer feel especially nervous about public speaking. This "Plan a Tic" strategy allows you to work out your feelings in a minimally disruptive way; you can both release the nervousness and look your best.

It's great to play cat, to stretch and yawn, or to play scarecrow and swing your arms loosely around as though they were being flipped in the breeze. These exercises are guaranteed to make you feel better. But you can't do them in front of a group.

We suggest that you develop a nervous habit that will permit your body to let off steam, but which is less obtrusive than, say, compulsively adjusting your bra strap. Your nervous habit should be appropriate on a stage or in meetings when people are looking at you.

You can use slow exhalation breathing when you are being observed. You can also concentrate your nervous energy into one part of your body.

Experiment with pressing your thumb hard up against the side of the index finger next to it. Leave the rest of your fingers curling around naturally. One white thumb knuckle will show. In the meantime, your face is composed, your body posture is good and your mind is trained on whatever is happening in the group. This technique is a counterirritant. The principle is the same when you pinch yourself on the arm when the dentist's drill is whining. A cow's nose is grabbed painfully to distract the cow while it is being branded.

Some people dig one fingernail into the palm of the same hand. Other curl up the toes on one foot, confining muscular tensions to one spot.

You can pinch your earlobe with great force without hurting it or calling attention to yourself while you are seated at a desk or table. Yet this pressure gives your body a chance to let its nervousness "talk."

How Not to Relax

Alcohol doesn't work. A drink will fuddle your brain, your tongue, your vision and your balance. It will not steady your nerves. The combination of alcohol and adrenaline in your system can have unexpected and unpleasant side effects (like hives; this is not cute). Coffee will not sober you up. It only produces an awake drunk person—as any state trooper will attest.

If you are drinking anything stronger than water your liaison will worry that you may turn out like their speaker from three years ago, who was plastered by the time he was introduced. Your hosts want you to do well. Don't cause them unnecessary edginess by trying to dull your panic at the bar.

When the speaker joins the group in a cocktail at the pre-speech banquet, the group isn't consciously disapproving. In fact, if you ask, most people will look puzzled or claim to *prefer* that the speaker "has a little knock before she has to work, har har." There is usually, however, a silent under-current of expectation that you abstain.

Water is the best drink. A carbonated beverage may bring

on burping. If you are eating lightly before the speech, coffee can make you sick. Caffeine may stimulate you more than it usually does; combined with an oversupply of adrenaline it can give you an unpleasant "racy" feeling.

Lay Off the Pills. This is not the proper forum for statistics on women and drug abuse, particularly tranquilizers, or the "better living through chemistry" hype. Suffice it to say that your first stand-up presentation is the wrong time to begin experimenting with Librium. Even if you have a prescription for a mild tranquilizer and you know how it affects you, it may still be better to depend on yourself to avoid/recover from the symptoms of stage fright. Can you imagine anything more boring than a tranquil speaker?

Summary

To relax for a speech, to feel mentally ready and loose, requires about 75 percent preparation, 15 percent breathing technique, 5 percent exercises (outlined in this chapter) and 5 percent psyching yourself. Pills and booze rate 0 percent

You calm yourself best by relying on adequate preparation. Give yourself every edge, do yourself every favor, allow yourself every break. Don't saddle yourself with any concerns beyond the speech itself. Read Chapter Six and make sure you are *ready*.

When you have done all the constructive thinking you can do, all the problem-solving you can, forget it. Replace every anxious "What if ..." with your fantasy of yourself as Ms. Competent of the Western Hemisphere.

Fantasize success, including successful recovery. Psych yourself by seeing yourself do well, turning people on, feeling your words as you say them, looking self-assured. Hear yourself speaking in your best voice—full of life, at a pleasant pitch, and loud enough for all to hear. Keep this image in mind; enjoy the daydream.

Then do it. Speak up. Throw yourself vigorously into the

action you fear. Do it again and again. Solicit opportunities to get experience. Never let a meeting go by without making a contribution. Practice builds confidence. The mixed feelings of fear, relief, and satisfaction eventually become a genuine desire to communicate and participate. On the day you do an outstanding job you will know it and so will everyone who was listening. This is a thrill so addictive it can hook the most retiring novice.

Reduce the general fear in your life by trying related confidence-builders: find a feminist assertiveness training group. Talk back. Don't smile. Learn how to jump out of airplanes. When you feel yourself losing perspective, think about things that are really dangerous. Practice making yourself conspicuous. Walk down the aisles to sit at the front of lecture halls and movie theaters. Stay out of chairs in corners. Remember we fear fear itself.

> Cautious, careful people always casting about to preserve their reputation or social standards can never bring about a reform.
> SUSAN B. ANTHONY

CHAPTER FOUR

How to Arrange a Successful Speech

Most of the participants in Speaking Up[SM] workshops join the group thinking that they have never made a "speech" and probably never will. They take the course simply to improve themselves, to learn to present themselves effectively in all kinds of everyday situations. But before long it becomes clear that most of them *have* made speeches and will make many more. Whenever you give a report at a meeting, introduce a speaker, give instructions to a group, teach a class, or present an award, you are making a speech. The purpose of the next three chapters is to take the mystery out of giving a good speech. The advice is applicable to every speech whether it is long or short, widely heard or for a few. We will take you through everything you need to know, step by step. The "secrets" are simple but they take a while to explain and to read. Naturally, we don't expect you to ever do *all* the "do's" or avoid all the "don'ts"—nobody ever has—but we've tried to make sure that they are all here.

Whether your presentation is at a small meeting, in a panel discussion, at an outdoor rally or to the General Assembly of the United Nations, we consider it a "formal" speech if you are given time to prepare it. The advance warning (*not* the size of the audience, the seriousness of the occasion or the length of the talk) distinguishes a "formal" speech from an "impromptu" (see Chapter Nine). Many inexperienced speakers seem to believe that there is something wrong with careful serious preparation and especially with using extensive notes. We cannot overemphasize how mistaken this notion is. While there are occasions on which you have to speak without preparation and occasions when you choose to speak without notes, they are very rare. A competent performance demands preparation, rehearsal and good notes.

At first, it might seem that the first step in preparing a speech would be to write it. Not so. Before you can write an effective speech you have to know for what audience it is being written. What is the situation? What kind of speech should it be? What is the purpose of your speech?

An informative speech is an extended answer to a question. For example, speeches with titles like "A Brief History of the Women's Movement in England" or "Food Cooperatives and How They Work" or "The Employee Benefit Program and How to Use It" are probably informative.

A persuasive speech is one that tries to get the audience to take action, to think or to do something. It is usually informative as well, but because you care about convincing your audience you will invest more of your beliefs, personality, values and emotions in a persuasive presentation. Academic texts on public speaking often make precise distinctions between one kind of speaking and another. We think this is silly. You almost never tell anyone anything without also trying to get her to apply, interpret or experience the information in a certain perspective—yours.

To persuade, you must work with the motivations of your audience, find out what is likely to sway them. It is not enough to inform the audience of the *features* (information) of a course of action. You must also describe the *benefits* of the action to those you wish to persuade. People act on your recommendations only if they think it's in their interest to do so. People will listen to almost anything if it is entertaining, but won't *do* anything unless they believe it will get them something.

You must also find out what it is that people don't want to hear, what they object to, and address (not ignore) these objections in a persuasive talk.

Different audiences turn on to different things. The trick is to figure out what these things are. In general, people who pride themselves on being hardheaded realists (business people, scientists, engineers, etcetera) respond to facts, while those who think of themselves as humanitarians or intuitive or good with people will respond to emotions.

However, the smaller the group, the less effective a direct appeal to emotions will be. People in small audiences feel more like individuals than members of a large group do, and the "herd" response of a crowd to a direct appeal to feelings (sympathy, patriotism, outrage) may be missing.

Your speeches will be better written and more interestingly presented if you care and show that you care about your subject. If you believe that your ideas and recommendations are important, that belief will be contagious. Unfortunately, women are not always able to muster that self-confidence initially. It doesn't matter. Speaking out is intrinsically self-assertive, and as you learn to do it and do it effectively, your self-confidence, your faith in your own ideas will grow. Eventually you may become a brilliant speaker. In the meantime, when you sit down to put together a presentation, ask yourself: "Why do I care and why should others care?"

Ask Your Liaison Person to Help

The woman or man who is serving as your contact person with the group can be a tremendously effective ally. She (or he) not only invites, greets and pays you, she can also be your link to the audience in other ways. You can and should *use* the person, pose the right questions and ask for her help. She has an investment in your performance, so whether your liaison is your supervisor at work or a stranger, she will probably be more than willing to find out for you what you need to know. The following sections contain suggestions for using a liaison person's energy to your mutual advantage. You may also be a liaison person yourself from time to time and these tips will help you assist the speakers *you* work with to do a good job.

The length of your presentation, the complexity of the issues you present, and the approach you take will depend on the answers to the following questions:

What is the occasion for which you are gathered and will the general atmosphere be solemn or light? Will the audience expect instruction or entertainment?

Exactly what are they expecting you to talk about? It isn't unheard of for a speaker to unwittingly deliver a presentation on the exact same subject this group heard at their luncheon meeting last year—or last month.

If necessary, ask if you can have the speech changed to a subject closer to what you already know a lot about. For example, if they want you to discuss the peculiarities of dog behavior, and you are experienced only with collies (or with cats), have the topic changed.

The question to pose to yourself isn't "What should I talk about?" but "What do I *want* to talk about?"

How much does the audience already know about your topic? Most of us give speeches at work. We present an aspect of, problem with or solution for a business concern to people who already know a great deal about our subject.

If you deliver a paper at a conference, your colleagues may not know exactly what you're going to talk about but they know the field. The same is true when you deliver a report to a club or charitable organization.

In situations where audience members are not your colleagues, you must find out how much they know. Is there agreement among group members on the issues? Do not make assumptions about what people may know, or may believe. Ask your liaison.

Never condescend to an audience. Try not to tell people things they already know, ask them to do what they are already doing or think about something they've struggled with for years. Nobody was ever insulted by a speaker who assumed too much about her brains, open-mindedness or compassion. It is better to overestimate your audience than to infuriate them.

Are they looking forward to hearing you, or are they being forced to attend (e.g., a class or compulsory training workshop)?

Will they have been drinking? People who are half lit can't concentrate. You might want to shorten your talk, or be prepared to delete sections of it once underway. People who are on the way down from an alcoholic high tend to feel headachy and grouchy. Be brief and resolve not to take their irritation personally.

Will people be drifting in and out while you talk? If you aren't prepared for a casual coming and going and a bit of noise at the exits, you may become unduly nervous when people "walk out on you."

Will they be in a rush to leave? If you speak just before a lunch break when everyone is hungry or if you are the final speaker before the crowd rushes off to a gala party, you may want to keep it extra short. An audience in a giddy, anticipatory mood may not be very receptive to a serious talk.

What other speakers has this group heard? Who was the last speaker? How did they react to her/him? If Flo Kennedy or Art Buchwald appeared the week before, don't be heartbroken if you are a bit of a letdown by contrast; some speakers are very hard acts to follow. On the other hand, if the previous speaker put the group to sleep with a disappointing, overly technical address about the fish in Lake Michigan, you may seem dramatic and wonderful by comparison.

Is this usually a responsive group? How much do they ordinarily react? If you have been alerted ahead of time that the group is shy or apathetic, you can plan your talk accordingly. We tend to overreact to what people "think" of us. Don't imagine you are a failure if the applause is only perfunctory or if you have to use every trick in Chapter Seven to get them to participate or to ask questions.

During conversation with your liaison person, ask her if there's anything (a tragedy, a howlingly funny incident) that has happened lately. You don't want inadvertently to trigger either embarrassment or hysteria with the wrong joke or anecdote.

Assess Your Audience

You need information about audience members in order to persuade them. Don't jump to conclusions; the idea is to be prepared but flexible. Although no group of people is ever exactly as you might expect, you can make some good guesses. The answers to the following questions may influence what you say and how you say it.

What is the age range?
What is the educational background of most of the audience?
What is the economic status of the group?
Will it be a racially mixed group?
What are their politics?
What will the male/female ratio be?

Be sure to find out what the audience will be wearing in order to decide what to wear yourself.

You may want to select your outfit to shock them, or to "underwhelm" them if they're threatened by you. You might want to wear a Greek festival costume if you're speaking about ethnic dance. As a general rule of thumb, however, find out what the audience will be wearing and then wear something yourself that is just a trifle dressier than their clothes. The idea is to establish yourself as "The Speaker," to set yourself slightly apart from the crowd, to show them that you are taking their invitation seriously enough to dress up a little for them, and yet to look enough like them to establish yourself as a person they can identify with. For example, if you are going to talk to a high school class, the liaison (probably a teacher or student) will inform you that most of the audience will be in blue jeans. You may then elect to wear casual slacks and an ordinary (though not beat-up) sweater.

It's difficult enough to get through an audience's prejudices about your topic. Try not to dress in a way that will trigger their stereotypes about you. If your clothing style is unconventional (or will seem so to your audience) you may have to decide which battles you want to fight—or, rather, how many you want to fight at the same time.

An audience may not want to listen to you if you irritate their notions of how a proper or "real" woman looks and dresses. You run the risk of siphoning off energy better spent on your topic itself. You may engender a *new* controversy by under- or overdressing according to your group's norms, when you want the topic to be the sole controversy or object of attention.

On the other hand, you may feel that it's a sellout to give a talk in a flowered print shirtwaist if you haven't worn one in years. Sexy clothes, that is "sexy" as defined by *Cosmopolitan* magazine or *Playboy*, are always a bad idea. Both men and other women find them distracting. Dark glasses (sunglasses) harm the two-way live current of person-to-people contact you need.

We are not suggesting that you change who you are, but rather that you be aware of the possible reactions of the group to your clothes so that you won't be floored. You may regard your outfit as a costume, a part of an acting strategy to achieve the effect you want.

As you are writing your talk, try to assess what will touch the personal welfare of the individuals you will address. Determine your overall approach according to their preconceived notions about your topic. Most audiences, of course, are neutral or generally sympathetic.

Hostile audiences. If the information you have gleaned from your liaison indicates that the audience may be hostile to you personally, hostile to the measures you advocate or hostile to the group you represent, your speech must emphasize beliefs and experiences you have in common with that audience. Otherwise the audience will not believe you understand or care about their concerns and will disregard what you say.

Honor, do not ignore, the opinions of others when you compose your talk. Acknowledge by statement or clear implication the significant opinions of your audience. But don't take for granted that an audience will be hostile. If you do, you will be likely to be angry before you even arrive. No matter what the evidence, an audience should be assumed friendly until proven hostile. Be ready for anything, but don't burden yourself with a big chip on your shoulder.

Apathetic audiences. If you anticipate that the members of the group will be tired or uncomfortable or that they didn't want to come to hear you in the first place, then you must write a talk that will surprise them out of their lethargy or irritation. Startling statements and vivid illustrations are especially important if the group is bored. To intensify interest in you and your topic, present your information in as novel a way as you can. Look for fresh angles, words and examples that will jar them out of their complacency. You may have to lead off with your strongest material. Arousing curiosity, using humor, accenting the unusual and creating mystery are your antidotes to their ennui. Drama is important for apathetic groups, but remember that a hostile group wants evidence and reasoning.

Remember, we are not recommending that you become a chameleon. Your ideas, values and experience are unique and important. Obtaining information ahead of time helps you feel psychologically prepared and may help with the way you express your ideas, but it isn't going to cause you to change, and it shouldn't. If it helps you understand and have compassion for an audience to consider what they want, believe and care about, then you will be more persuasive. If you are trying to adopt an entirely new persona, or sugar-coat your unpopular convictions, you'll feel phony and it won't work.

Now, before you sit down to write, make sure you have cleared all of the arrangements with your liaison. Here is our checklist:

> *How large is the group?* Few things are more dreadful than preparing oneself for an armchair chat around a fireside and finding a crowd of five hundred gathered, or vice versa.

> *Time.*
>> *What time should you arrive?* If you want to arrive early to check the microphone, lights, etcetera, will somebody be there to meet you and unlock doors for you? What's the name of the person who will greet you?

>> *What time are you supposed to begin speaking?*

>> *Will you be expected to spend informal time with the group?* Do they want you to circulate and meet people? Will there be some sort of reception and/or do they want you to remain after your talk to chat with people informally? Do they expect you to do anything (sign autographs, have a meal) prior to the speech? Who will sit next to you at dinner, on the dais?

How long are you supposed to talk? How long do speakers usually talk to this group?

Will you be "onstage" for a long time before you speak? Your decision about shoes, short versus long skirt or slacks may be influenced by whether you will be seated or standing while you are on view and by how long you will be "sized up" before you speak.

Format. What is the overall schedule for the day? Who will speak before you? After you? Are you expected to entertain questions after your presentation? For how many minutes? Must you acknowledge anyone in your opening?

Guests. If this is an affair to which speakers are expected to bring a spouse, or Significant Other, where will she/he sit? On the dais with you? If your guest is a member of the other sex, what are the men wearing?

If the invitation to speak does not specify guests, would it be all right to bring a friend anyway? You may want to invite somebody who can help you evaluate what went right/wrong afterwards, and who will give you moral support.

Team speaking. If you are invited to solo, would they be willing to take two of you? A team speech is a great idea if you are nervous and would feel calmer if the chores can be shared; if the subject is controversial and another person would lend credibility to your viewpoint; if two personalities and styles might help offset the audience's tendency to stereotype a representative of your issue.

Directions to the site of the speech are vital. If you get the wrong room number in a huge classroom building you may waste precious time. How long does it take to get there? Should you allow extra time for the hour of the day? Will there be holiday traffic?

Transportation. Are they going to send someone to pick you up? If you are to be met at the airport how will you recognize your driver and where will you meet?

Parking. Where can you park, and how much will it cost?

Honorarium and expenses. Will you be paid? How much? When? To whom do you want the check made out?

If you plan to contribute the honorarium you have requested to a charity or to the organization you are representing, perhaps you would like your introducer to mention it. If there is a program printed for audience members, ask to have your contribution mentioned in it.

Will you be reimbursed for travel expenses (taxi, gas mileage)? Do they want receipts? If you are speaking at no charge, perhaps it would be appropriate to set up "collection baskets" at the exits with a request for contributions for your expenses or for the organization on whose behalf you are speaking.

Do not sell yourself short. If the group usually pays for speakers, don't volunteer to speak for free or for any amount less than the fair market value established by the group. Many people are saddled with the illusion that women can afford to give away their time, talents and expertise. There are a great many people who are more than willing to exploit women with the argument that we crave fulfillment and that monetary compensation is not the proper reward for our efforts. Forget the clichés about the beauty and moral edification of giving of oneself, the need to be needed, the therapeutic and self-fulfilling value of volunteering as a counterforce in a materialistic and self-seeking world. Leave the Lady Bountiful number to somebody who can afford to practice charity.

Precise financial arrangements should always be confirmed in writing.

Publicity. Any advertising (in-house memo, flyers and posters, radio announcements, etcetera) should be cleared with you for content. If your liaison person is inexperienced, perhaps you could suggest publicity as a way of attracting an audience. Supply a sheet of biographical information and/or information regarding your topic. Also ask your liaison to clip and send you copies of flyers, newspaper articles and the like for your records.

Introduction. Who will introduce you? Will you have an opportunity to talk to that person (in person, on the phone or through letters) to get some idea about what she plans to say and to give her suggestions? (See Chapter Eight.)

Seating. Will you be on stage, or in a banquet room or a conference room? Will your audience be seated in rows, or in a circle? You will want to request two things: the most intimate setting possible for the number of people you will be talking to (you just look goofy standing at a podium in front of a mike if there are only twelve people in the auditorium); and a way to refer to your notes that is convenient and does not seem pretentious in the setting.

Keep in mind that you want to be situated so that everyone can see and hear you. Depending on the size of the group, this may mean going to the front, or standing up (even though the other speakers stayed seated) or being seated on a platform higher than the audience. If you can see to it that the chairs are arranged in a semicircle or a circle for a small group, or concentric circles for a larger group, you can achieve a warmer atmosphere than you can when nobody can see anyone else.

Ask for a straight-backed chair for yourself. You will feel more in command, sit up straighter and probably be at a higher level (so that you can be seen easily) than those who sit in soft and comfy armchairs.

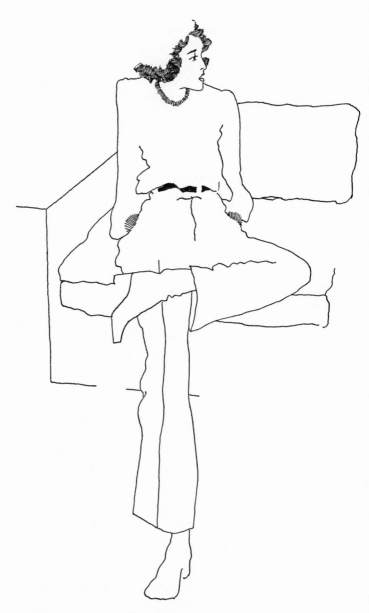

If you *must* sit on a sofa, don't melt into it.

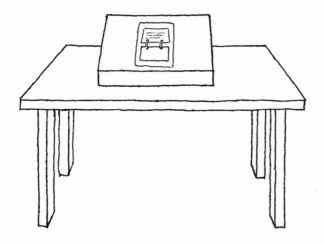

Take nothing for granted. If you are expecting to speak at a lectern and *they* expect you to rise and talk at your place, you may be unnerved.

Podium. If you are particularly tall, or short, ask how high the podium is or how high the table and table lectern, taken together, will reach.

You may need to request different equipment if the audience isn't going to be able to see your face over the rostrum. Suggest a box of a specified height, width and strength to stand on, or substitute a table with a table lectern. Note that most liaisons don't think about things like tablecloths. Your legs show whether you are seated or standing. This is important to remember for panel presentations when you are on view for a long time before your return to speak. If your face registers serenity and your legs are twisted into Syrian cheese strings, you will give a double message to the audience. You may also prefer trousers or a long skirt in these circumstances.

Sometimes speakers' tables are very long, with a mike at each place. Other times participants have to share a mike, passing it back and forth to take turns speaking. Sometimes there is just one mike, freestanding, and speakers must rise and go to it in order to talk.

If you are going to be using an antique podium, carved

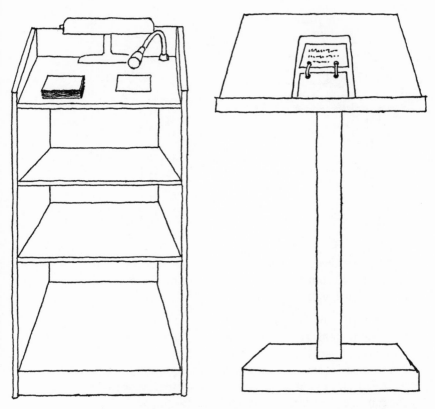

of mahogany in the days when 5'4" was considered tall for a man, and you stand 5'10", see if you can arrange a substitute. You don't want to have to bow from the waist every time you wish to refer to your cue cards.

Will you be miked? Your arrival time may depend on whether you want to do a mike check.

Questions and answers. One of the most important ways in which a liaison person can help you is in Q & A arrangements. She can solicit written but unsigned questions from audience members ahead of time. She can promise to ask a question if hands don't shoot up immediately. She can "plant" another questioner in the audience if the group is unusually shy or unresponsive. (See Chapter Seven.)

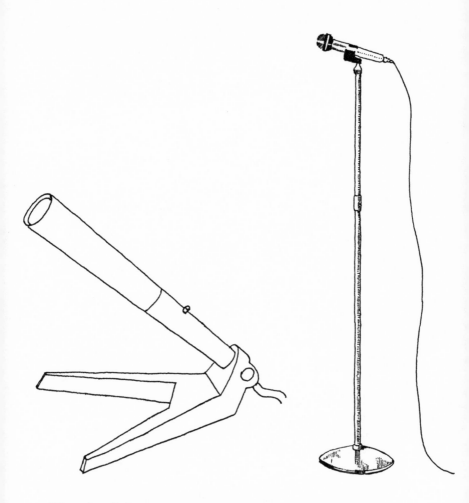

Time signals. Prearrange time signals with your liaison so you will know when your time is running out. Many speakers like to set up three signals: five minutes to go (hand up with five fingers spread wide); wrap it up, hurry (rolling arms in a football official's "illegal motion" signal); and time's up (forming a "T" with the hands).

The liaison can stand at the back of the room throughout your presentation to do this for you and also to signal you any time your voice drops so low that you become inaudible. If the liaison person can't do this, ask her to make arrangements with someone else sitting at the rear.

You must still use a watch with a large face and large numerals and hands. Arrangements can break down.

Visual aids, handouts. If you are going to use a projector, hand out printed material, etcetera, the arrangements must be absolutely clear. Do you want to pass out a mimeo to everyone in the audience at a particular moment in your talk? Then the liaison person can arrange to have "runners" ready to distribute them quickly and efficiently on a signal from you. Do you want someone to stand near the lights so that when it's time to show your slides there will be no awkward delay?

Water. Don't assume that everyone knows that a speaker appreciates having at least a cup of the stuff on hand. Ask for it.

Tape recorder. Could some kind soul tape your talk on the recorder you're bringing so you can hear it later?

Remember, the liaison wants you to be a hit. In our experience, liaisons are often much more nervous than speakers, and appreciate it if you value their role as facilitators. Don't let the liaison's nerves infect *you!* Reassure her by knowing just what you need and radiating confidence.

All of this probably seems like a lot of trouble. Actually, it takes a lot longer to talk about than to do. Give yourself the best possible chance for success by making sure that nothing will distract from your fabulous speech. For how to write that fabulous speech, read on.

CHAPTER FIVE

Writing to Be Heard

Writing a speech, even a very short one, is hard work, particularly if you haven't tried it before. In addition to the difficulties most of us have writing anything, there are specific problems with speech writing. Unlike literature, oral style is not for beauty or permanence. The effect of the moment is what counts. Writing to be heard is different from writing to be read. A great speech may read badly and a bad speech may be easy to read.

Why Is Speech Writing Different?

When people read, they reread. Watch someone read a newspaper article, and you will notice that her eyes drift back up from time to time to reread sentences or whole paragraphs. She would not have this advantage if she were listening. When we listen we have only one chance to understand. Rhetorical devices such as repetition are used not only to heighten the drama of a speech but also to compensate for the fact that the audience cannot reread significant passages.

This is also the reason long complex sentences are usually inappropriate, why technical information, especially numbers, should be carefully spaced and repeated, and why foreign phrases, unusual or unfamiliar titles and so forth should be clearly enunciated, spoken slowly or if necessary explained.

You use punctuation when you write (italics, bold type, capital letters, etcetera) to let the reader know what is important, what she should stop to think over before moving on. When you talk you don't punctuate. You must use inflection, pauses, and pacing to make your points.

Oral language, in short, requires more repetition and simpler sentence structure than written language. Short, terse sentences may bother a reader, but not a hearer.

Begin at Once

Preparation for a speech is at least 50 percent rehearsal. You are both playwright and the cast—don't neglect the second phase. Begin to jot down ideas the minute you agree to give a talk. Blank paper is terrifying. The longer you wait, the more difficult it is, and almost any beginning is better than none. As soon as you accept the invitation to speak, start making notes on tissue, napkins, tatty pieces of paper, or best of all a notebook you carry. If you panic and speech ideas don't come, then start out by writing "The purpose of this speech is..." or "I think I will write about...," "In general, I will discuss...," "I especially want to emphasize..." until you are ready to start thinking about communicating to them, those people you have agreed to talk to.

Feel Communicative

As you begin, think about your audience. Intensify your interest and impulse to communicate. Write *to* them, remembering that "they" are not a monolith. An audience is one person, then another, then another. We *talk* with one another. Try to feel this way as you begin your first draft. It will help you to establish a tone for your speech—light or serious, warm or intense or sincere or funny—to think about whom the speech is for, and how you can tell it best to *them*.

Try rereading some of your old speeches, or John Bartlett's *Familiar Quotations*, to put yourself in a speech writing frame of mind. The most important step may be putting yourself into the proper spirit. If necessary, think of someone *else* doing the speech. What would her objectives be?

The First Draft

About 80 percent of what your speech will eventually include should come off the top of your head in the first draft. Keeping your audience in mind, begin to rough out ideas. What is your point? Write down, in stream of consciousness style, everything you think you might want to say. Don't lose any ideas; you can edit later. Don't worry about grammar or spelling or scintillating language or organization or being perfect or even being good. Just get thoughts on paper. Write until you've worn out your information supply. It is easier to edit a mishmash of material than to create from scratch. That's why there are more good editors than good writers. Just get something in front of you—everything will be easier from then on.

When your first draft notes are finished you are ready to fill in the gaps with research. Research does not mean learning a whole subject area and then trying to write a speech about it. When we say "research" we mean checking quotations or statistics for accuracy, or reading the newest material on your topic to make sure your information is current, or rereading source material to refresh your memory.

As a general guideline, refuse a speaking engagement if you must spend more than 20 percent of your preparation time on research. If you aren't utterly familiar with your subject, your self-confidence will be undermined. Most of your preparation time should be divided between editing and rehearsing. Again, 80 percent of the things you say should be things you already knew, things that came off the top of your head in the first draft.

Don't trust your memory; carry a notebook. At every stage of speech writing and editing, ideas, turns of phrase and lines of reasoning will occur to you, often at odd times. Relaxed moments when you seem to be doing nothing (riding an elevator, waiting in a line) are often times of high creativity. Your subconscious is full of good information that likes to escape when you are lost in thought staring into the refrigerator. Jot down your ideas and save them. If you love your topic, you will dash off a great many more quips and quotes than you will be able to use ... for *this* speech. If your subject bores you (and many work-related presentations may), it is even more important to let your imagination loose. A fresh approach to dull material will often occur to you *only* when you are free from the constraints of official "writing" and doing something mundane like brushing your hair.

Writers, filmmakers, strategists in business and politics often share a nocturnal quirk: they *use* the moments between sleeping and waking because these are unusually productive times for the imagination. Instead of getting a good idea, rolling over to snooze and forgetting the idea by the next day, try keeping pencil and notebook by your bed. You may have to scrawl in the dark, but you won't lose the idea. You also may develop insomnia, but only for the duration.

After you have finished your first draft and you have moved on to the research stage, abandon the writing for as long as you dare—several days if you have a week to write it, several weeks if you have a month. You may not think about the talk in your conscious mind very often, but your subconscious will take over for you. Speech writing is like any other kind of writing; it benefits from latent periods, from lying fallow for a stretch of time. After a "fermenting" period you can return to your notes with a fresh perspective—new phrases, notes you've been compiling, research you have completed. Because your subconscious mind has been composing the speech all along, you will have a much clearer understanding of what you want to say and your second draft will seem almost effortless.

The Second (etcetera) Draft

Instead of rewriting or retyping your speech each time you revise it, experiment with "cutting and pasting." Much editing consists of reorganizing ideas into a different order; retyping may not be the most efficient method. Cross out sentences you don't like, type new ones on clean paper, and tape them over the old ones. Rearrange the sequence of your talk by scissoring out paragraphs and taping or stapling them where you think they might fit better. A photostat or Xerox copy of the resulting page is easy to work from.

Editing a speech differs from editing material intended to be read because you want to know not only if it is well organized and clear but also how it sounds.

The best way to find out is to read each draft into a tape recorder. When you listen to your speech objectively you can ask: Does it have variety? Is it easy to understand? Is it interesting? Is the pace too fast or slow? Does it sound warm and friendly or cold and flat? Do I *like* that woman?

Editing Your First Draft for Organization

The rule is to make positively, unequivocally certain that you have a point and that you state it so clearly that every person leaving the hall will be able to give a concise, coherent synopsis of your presentation. "Uh, she talked about baseball" is not good enough.

Several generations ago, two hour orations were commonplace. Today, a twenty minute "conversation enlarged" is the norm. So don't be too ambitious. In a five-minute talk you can make one major point; in a twenty minute talk you can only make two. The most common, and fatal, speech-writing mistake is trying to say too much. It is better to have one theme, stated powerfully and memorably, than to ramble around six points. Be strict with yourself when you make the final decision about what you plan to cover. We recognize that it is difficult to do this, especially if you know a great deal about your topic. Simplifying in many cases seems like falsifying. Alas, you must make choices. (It helps to remember that if you put in too much your audience won't remember it anyway.)

Here are the steps to rewriting your first draft:

Reread your first draft and see if you know what your point is. This sounds like we are being funny but the major cause of confused disjointed unclear speech writing is confused disjointed unclear thinking. The reason most first drafts are such a mess is that the writer really doesn't know what she thinks and why until after she has written stuff down and tried it out. The process of trying to make our thoughts clear on paper sometimes helps us see that they aren't such hot thoughts in the first place.

Make an outline. Outline your own speech as if you were taking notes from a stranger's speech. Pick out the major points and subsidiary points of what this person is trying to say. Now rearrange the outline so it is clear and easy to follow.

Write a new speech from the outline using as much of the old stuff as is salvageable. (These steps take a long time if you are new at speech writing, so start early.)

Certain topics lend themselves logically to chronological or sequential organization (e.g., organizing a conference, how to repair a carburetor, the story of your life). This is fine as long as you are careful to vary your language and rhythm and not give a speech on the Legislative History of the Equal Rights Amendment that goes like this. "In 1970 women gathered...In 1971 there were some changes..., in 1972 Congress..." Also avoid saying, "First, you take your complaint

form to the Equal Employment Opportunity Commission...
Second, you attempt to conciliate the charge with your
employer... Third, you obtain a 'right to sue' letter..."
These kinds of transitions are too repetitious.

Persuasion organization, or how to make a mad idea seem
plausible:

1. Opening. Secure attention of audience. Rivet them
   with a ringing phrase.
2. State the problem. Color it with an anecdote or a
   quotation.
3. Prove the existence of the problem. Use statistics,
   quotations and examples.
4. Describe the unfortunate consequences of the problem or prevailing conditions. How do these consequences affect this audience? Persuade them to be
   concerned. Make them feel personally dissatisfied
   with the way things are.
5. Is there a solution? What changes does the audience
   fear? What changes does it desire?
6. State your solution. Document why it is the most
   effective solution.
7. Show how your solution will benefit the audience
   and paint a glowing picture of how life will be once
   your idea has been enacted. "Sales, particularly in the
   south and southwest, should increase 15 percent in the
   first six months and go on increasing steadily."
   Stress the advantages for this audience of the bene-
   ficial changes you suggest.
8. Anticipate and answer the objections you know are
   coming.
9. Invite action. This is the climax of your speech.
   Appeal to their motives (pleasure? advancement?
   sympathy? pride? loyalty? fear?).

The tone of your speech may be angry, hopeful, concilia-
tory or all three. In any case, be wary of bullying people,
getting their backs up.

The objective is to create dissatisfaction with the way things are, or to bring the dissatisfaction that is lurking under the surface up to awareness. Don't create resistance—an audience is persuaded best if you can convince them they figured out the solution by themselves.

Remember that you want to get on strong and get off strong. Pay particular attention to your opening remarks and your conclusion. Most amateur speakers overwrite their opening. Avoid making it too strong to keep up with as you go along. Also avoid being more personal with the audience at first than they are ready to accept. The impression your opening should give is of a pleasant knowledgeable person who is beginning to talk to the audience. The conclusion, on the other hand, can be as dramatic as you like. It may be all the audience remembers, so make it memorable. A strong ringing ending, "Give me liberty or give me Death," is not the only way to do this. The final sentence can be delivered with quiet sincerity yet leave the listeners at an emotional high point.

Editing for Style

There are three main points to remember when you edit for style:

1. There is *no* subject that cannot be made interesting.
2. This is a speech, not an essay. Write something you can *feel* while you say it.
3. This is a conversation, even though only one person is talking. You want to sound like yourself, not a book.

If you write an article or an essay (instead of a speech) you get stuck delivering your article or essay out loud to the audience. If you want the speech to have a conversational, sharing, making-friends tone, you will have to write in it. If you want people to feel talked with (not at or to) you will have to write it that way. A one-to-one quality cannot come from your delivery alone.

The following suggestions will help you avoid a grim, turgid, nonoral talk:

Don't say the title.   Speech titles or topics are for publicity for the printed program or for the introducer to announce.

Skip the fillers.   Greetings such as "Good afternoon, ladie and gentlemen" aren't necessary. Jump right in with you first line.

"Thank you" is too often a filler. If you have some reasor to say it (a nice introduction merits a turn of the head anc thank you to the introducer, or a round of applause require: a thanks to the audience), go ahead. But remember thai women have suffered from the female socialized "gratefuls' and "humbles" quite long enough. We frequently put our-selves down by confusing submissive language with courtesy.

See if you can throw away the introductory paragraph and start with the sentences that sound involved, invested, ex-cited and emotionally "there." You want to begin naturally and as if you were talking among friends. Most of the pomposity, arch jokes and phony "attention getters" are probably in your first paragraph. Cut them.

Avoid generalizations.   The more you generalize the more you are likely to say something that is not true or to offend. Don't say "Women think" if you mean "The Black women at Vassar in 1975 indicated on a survey..." The more specific you are the less likely you are to be wrong.

Don't make lists.   The following is an example of list-making that may be fine for an article, but will *not* work in a speech:

> If you are concerned about family violence and want to know what to do, how to start a refuge for battered wives... my advice is to start at the local level: form coalitions and task forces; research applicable state laws and city ordinances;

investigate policies and procedures for law enforcement (police, district attorney, and the courts); gather statistics from every conceivable source; canvass emergency housing and note admission policies; determine what services are already available and which need to be established; draw up proposals based on that information; make funding agencies aware of the need; lobby for remedial legislation at every level of government; demand a reordering of priorities in government and foundation spending; and don't stop until all necessary programs are realized.*

There is absolutely no way you could deliver those ideas without sounding as though you were reading a shopping list. Your voice will get sing-songy and monotonous. The ideas will have to be rewritten for a speech to eliminate the sameness that is bound to creep into the delivery.

Use concrete examples. If you want to talk about day care, tell a story about one family that illustrates your point. If you want to discuss hunger in the United States, use a composite person to illustrate your facts. (For example, "George Carver lives in Appalachia. He is six years old. George eats chalk, paste and grass. He can't pay attention in school because he's starving . . .") Your audience will respond more attentively to a case history than they can to the information that many people in this country are hungry and undernourished.

If you talk about drought conditions in Africa, make your facts come alive by telling how drought affects one tribe. If you are explaining urban transportation, tell an anecdote about one person who can't get from her home to her job. Audiences have a hard time getting charged up over an abstract concept or a rhetorical generalization.

Use active voice. Make the subject of each sentence act. Your speech goes flat if the action is happening *to* someone or something.

---

* The ideas for this example were taken from Del Martin, *Battered Wives.*

Wrong Passive Voice	Right Active Voice
It has occurred to me, It seems to me	I think, I believe
The bomb is dropped by the airplane.	The pilot bombed the village and killed the people.
It is thought	The Board said
Women are denied equal pay	The vice president of personnel denied equal pay to women
The problem to be investigated	Our committee will investigate

Check your verbs for color. Read through the whole speech and replace every dull verb with one that expresses the precise shade of action you want to convey. Use a thesaurus or dictionary. For instance, why say "I walked in" if you really strolled, wandered, dashed or lurched? Beware of the verbs to have, to be and got. If you *have* a cold, a drink or a hard time, you aren't *sick* with a cold, *gulping* a drink or *struggling*. If you pick the right verb you don't need four adverbs.

Use visual language. Help the audience make movies in their heads while you talk. For example:

"Students pay a yearly athletic fee."
vs.
"Students pull the athletic fee from their jeans each year."

"It's just trading one set of problems for another, not solving them."
vs.
"It's just rearranging the deck chairs on the *Titanic*."

Avoid extended metaphors. Comparisons are great, but please, no "ship of state foundering on the rocks of insolvency after a rough sea of fiscal irresponsibility crying for a new captain with a new economic mandate as the lighthouse to guide us into a harbor . . ."

The longer you stretch a comparison, the harder it becomes to make two ideas or objects match up. Maybe you can prove that a girl is like a rose in a hundred ways—but why bother?

Statistics

Space them. Audiences cannot absorb more than two or three numbers or percentages at a time. Even when you read them, large numbers are meaningless until you stop to think about them, to visualize what they connote. Numbers are even harder to hear than to read. Spread out any numerical information and pad it with English.

Repeat them. It's harder to remember numbers than words. Radio announcers repeat the phone number for call-ins dozens of times in an hour. Repeat key statistics.

Make them visual. An audience can grasp the visual significance of a football field better than they can the concept of "100 yards." If you explain that something is the size of a cockroach, your image will have more impact than a measurement in centimeters. Don't just tell us how many feet tall something is, compare it in size to an object we are familiar with—a downtown skyscraper, a telephone booth, your podium.

"Americans spend an average of thirteen hours per year on civic or community improvements."

vs.

"The average American spends more time each year putting on underarm deodorant than on improving the community."

"According to conservative estimates, 255,000 rape incidents will occur in the U.S. this year."

vs.

"Statistics show that a large percentage of the women in this room will be raped this year. There are about fifty of us, so counting off that would mean you, Kathy, and you, Georgia . . ."

"The federal government does have the funds to establish a new consumer protection agency. But the government has different priorities."

vs.

"A new consumer protection agency would cost on a yearly basis what the Pentagon spends in two hours."

Give the actual numbers when your talk demands precision and accuracy. You may still use a comparison afterward.

Suit them to the audience. To a group of Girl Scouts: "That means that the protein in a single hot dog is more than some kids eat in a whole week." To a group of successful business people: "The cost of one drink before lunch would supply milk for ten children for a week."

Jargon

Rehearse your speech with other people. You will be able to judge by their facial expressions whether the speech contains technical language or a special word that should be defined or edited out. Even when it is your own jargon and you're talking to your own colleagues, it's refreshing and often enlightening to try to speak English.

Clichés

If it sounds like something you've heard a hundred times, don't say it. We already know kites are high, foxes are sly, mules are stubborn and pride is justifiable. Rephrase anything that sounds hackneyed. (See Chapter Two.)

Can You Say It?

Can the audience hear the whole sentence? Or will they have forgotten the beginning of it by the time you have wound your way through all the commas and clauses and arrived at the end? Can you say the things that go together in one breath? Don't distort the sense of your phrases by having to pause for breath in the wrong places. Shorten your sentences if your delivery sounds choppy or uneven. Avoid alliteration (e.g., Peter Piper picked a peck of Pickled Peppers). Avoid phrases that might turn into something embarrassing if misspoken (e.g., seven sheet slitters slitting sheets). The only way to tell if this will happen is to *rehearse out loud.*

Doublecheck to make certain any difficult concept or central argument is repeated often enough. Make it clear when you move from one point to the next. Be sure, if you have promised three main points, to deliver three.

Speech is *talk*, so say "she's, they're, don't, can't." "She is, they are, do not, cannot" sound too formal unless you are pronouncing the words out in full to emphasize them.

Is It YOU?

Does the speech sound like something you would say on a good day? Can you carry it off or is there something in it that might trip you up or embarrass you? Delete anything that doesn't feel "right." An elegant passage that would earn high marks in the *Times* literary supplement may *sound* ridiculous. If you have found a poem that states exactly what you want to convey, think twice before you use it. If you are not an actress, if you have never tried to recite poetry before, if you feel uncomfortable saying the words (much as you love to read them silently to yourself), skip it. This is also true of slang, even mild obscenity, descriptions of bodily functions, sexual allusions and many "jokes." If you can't carry it off, leave it out.

Quotations

Audiences love quotes, but you undercut their effectiveness if you present them clumsily. Avoid saying "quote ... unquote." Instead, use inflection to indicate that you are quoting, or you can introduce the quotation by saying:

"...," said Polly Grant, "is. ..."
Barbara Anthony expressed her advice on ... in this way: "..."
Alan Hewat has said, "..."
"..." (using strong inflection). In those words, attorney
Suzanne Stocking expressed ...

Sometimes you don't want to quote someone directly, but you wish to acknowledge that the ideas you are expressing are not original. Try: "In considering ..., I've been greatly helped by Artemis March's brilliant theoretical analysis." Or, "Obviously, these notions have been influenced by Ralph Nader's work, especially *Unsafe at Any Speed*."

Avoid lengthy quotations; the audience came to hear *you*. Also, don't quote the same source over and over again. If your topic is sex, don't just stick to Masters and Johnson. Your four-year-old, Jayne Mansfield and *Our Bodies, Ourselves* by the Boston Women's Health Book Collective have had things to say, too.

Now you have a more or less final draft of your speech. Have you done what you set out to do? Do you like it? Good. The speech is ready to go onto your cue cards.

Good Notes

There are two ways that you can turn your final draft into useful cue cards. You can present the speech from the full text or you may prefer to speak from an outline.

Full text means that every word you have written appears in your notes and you intend to present these notes without deviation, asides or digressions. This system is best for speakers who are a bit nervous and don't want to leave anything to chance, for very formal situations where every word counts (such as testimony that will be a part of a record, or when the speech will be reprinted in the press or in a journal of proceedings) and, of course, for presenting a paper at a conference. (By the way, a speech belongs to you just as a story or poem would. We suggest you put "© copyright" and the year on your text.)

Detailed outline. For most occasions, however, it will seem comfortable to use a *detailed outline.* When a speaker works from an outline, she is prepared yet flexible. A detailed outline can maximize your spontaneity and interaction with the audience. "Full text" speakers must sometimes struggle to sound fresh. The audience has come to hear a talk, not a reading.

When you use an outline you must still write the speech out in full and rehearse it. Then you reduce it to a detailed outline. (You will rehearse the speech again from the outline before you deliver it.) Detailed means detailed. For example, the full text reads:

> People may hate their work, but even so they try to make something out of it. In factories and offices around this country work is systematically reduced to the most minute and repetitious tasks. Supervision ranges from counting bones, raising hands to use the bathroom, issuing "report cards" with number and letter grades for quantity, quality, cooperation, dependability, attendance, etc.
>
> Through all this workers make a constant effort, sometimes creative, sometimes pathetic, sometimes violent, to put meaning and dignity back into their daily activity.
>
> I realize now, much more deeply than ever, that work is a human need following right after the need for food and the need for love. The crime of modern industry is not forcing us to work, but denying us real work.*

Poor outline:

> People hate work, but try
> work reduced to minute
> supervision (examples)
> workers try to put dignity back

* Barbara Garson, *All the Livelong Day.*

work is human need
crime being denied real work

The above outline will not serve the speaker well for two reasons: first, she may misunderstand her own shorthand and state that "people hate to work so they try to reduce it"; secondly, much of the punch of the text may be lost if the speaker can't remember the examples of supervision she had planned to give, or the adjectives (pathetic, violent, creative) that describe the workers' efforts.

Detailed outline:

People may hate work, but they try make something
Factories, offices . . .
Work systematically reduced, repetitious tasks
Supervision: counting bones
               hands bathroom
               report cards—quantity
                             quality
                             attendance
Workers' constant effort—creative
                        pathetic
                        violent
   put meaning, dignity
Realize work human need . . . food . . . love
Crime not forcing . . . denying real work

The best outlines minimize the number of words running across the card and present instead a vertical list of topics going down the card. This arrangement isolates thoughts so that they are easy to pick up in sequence. Exaggerated punctuation helps, too.

Save Everything

Keep all your texts and outlines. Save your cue cards. It is even a good idea to keep research cards with groups of phrases or several ways of stating the same idea or fact. Out of this collection of old material you build the kind of file that helps you prepare more efficiently for each address. It shows you how you have experimented, what works and what doesn't for you. Furthermore, if you speak often on the same subject you'll be able to mix, match and toss together a new speech in a very short time from sections of old ones. This is called a *modular speech*.

Your Props: Text and Visual Aids

The rehearsal stage begins when you are satisfied with your text. You will put yourself at a great practical advantage, as well as a psychological one, if the good speech you have just written is delivered from legible cards that won't trip you up and that look like they belong to somebody who knows what she is doing. Sloppy notes can make you feel unprepared and disheveled, and they can make you feel embarrassed and uneasy if others see them.

Cue cards. Print your speech in large letters on 8″ x 5″ white unlined cards. These are larger than regular standard index cards. Use very wide margins and print no more than eight lines per card. This is no time to worry about the lumber shortage; use only one side of the card. For clarity, write with black felt-tip pen.

We prefer cue cards to paper for several reasons. The wind can blow paper away if you are speaking outdoors, or even indoors if a fan is blowing. It's easier to find your place if you have few lines and words to choose from when you look down. If your hands are shaking, it will be less conspicuous if you are holding heavy cards instead of rustling paper. If you are on a mike, cards make less noise. The reason for wide margins is that it is easy to find your place if you are reading down the page, not across.

If you feel you need more space, try cardboard shirt cards that come from the dry cleaners. Use wide margins, and print only on the top half of the cards. The blank bottom half will

```
TREAT  WORKERS  LIKE

CHILDREN  OR  POTENTIAL

ROBOTS.  IT  IS  THIS

TREATMENT  ——  MORE

THAN  THE  MEANINGLESS

OBJECTIONS  THAT  EMPLOYERS
```

O   O

help keep the text up high so you don't have to lower your head each time you glance at your notes.

Don't worry if you need a lot of cards, especially for your first few presentations when you are still learning how to abbreviate words.

Here is a sample of an unfinished cue card for a full text presentation, unabbreviated. It is incomplete because it has no stickers or other aids added yet. Notice that the punctuation is exaggerated. Try using long dashes for pauses (and obey them when you come to them!). Your punctuation doesn't have to be grammatically accurate, but it should be speech accurate. If you might pause too long at a grammatically correct comma, leave it out. If you are preparing script for a TelePrompTer, use dashes only.

Number the cards in the upper right.

Everything you put on the card must be readable from arm's length.

Abbreviate whenever you can. As you grow more familiar with your own "shorthand" you can abbreviate more and more for delivery. If you could remember in front of a firing squad that ♀ is the symbol for "woman," use it. But if you might forget it under pressure, write out the word instead.

Common abbreviations and symbols include:

∴ Therefore
2 Two, too or to
g Any "ing" ending (walkg 2 the store)

Eventually you can begin to delete articles (the, an, a) and most vowels and word endings. For example:

Full text:

> "In glancing through back issues of 'Womanpower' before coming to speak with you this evening, I noticed that there is a disproportionate number of complaints and suits based on sex discrimination filed in the state of Florida. I wondered if I had been invited to the land of sunshine or a lion's den."

Abbreviated text:

> "In glancg thru back iss of WP b4 comg 2 speak w/u this eve, I notcd theres a disproptnate # of C & S based on S. D. fild in state Fla. I wonderd if I had bn invitd 2 land of sunshn or a lion's den."

Once again, let us emphasize that you do not do this until you are sure you can. If you have any doubts, don't. Jane, for one, never abbreviates because she can't understand her own abbreviations under stress.

Never use real shorthand, even if you have been using it for years. Shorthand is like a foreign language. It requires translation in your head before you can speak the words out loud. Shorthand may confuse you in a tense moment.

Typed cards. If your presentation is longer than ten minutes you may want to type it. Printing is better than typing for short presentations because the act of printing itself is a memory aid. One generally remembers little of any text one copytypes.

If you type, use nothing but upper case letters and triple space between lines. Indent each paragraph *ten* spaces. Go back over the cards with a felt-tip pen after they are typed to enlarge your punctuation marks. Type size 29 is used by speech writers for governors and other people who must make presentations every day.

After you have rehearsed out loud several times from your text or outline on the cue cards, you will get a good idea about where to "decorate" the cards so that your delivery will go smoothly.

Number the cards.

Attach stickers on them for body language reminders. Stickers* are small white papers with sticky backing. They come in different shapes, and you can buy them at dime stores or stationery supply stores. They are used for *delivery reminders*, such as those illustrated on page 94.

Don't write words on your stickers. You might try to read "smile" instead of smiling. Draw a picture instead. It also helps to draw with a bright color on the stickers. New speakers complain that under stress they ignore their stickers. It takes practice to be able to deliver the text *and* make the adjustments your stickers remind you about.

Underline words you want to emphasize in a third color. For instance, use black for the text, red for the sticker pictures and green for the underlining.

Draw small down arrows ($\downarrow$) over your emphasis words. Adjectives, adverbs and the last word in a sentence should be emphasized down (with a lower pitch) rather than up.

---

* This idea, as far as we know, originated with Dorothy Sarnoff. Dorothy Sarnoff, *Speech Can Change Your Life*, Dell Publishing Company, Inc., New York, 1972.

SMILE

 STOP WAVING HANDS AROUND

 STOP FEET

 EYE CONTACT

 PITCH DOWN

 LOUDER

 PAUSE

 PAUSE, THEN SPEAK FASTER

 PAUSE, THEN SLOW DOWN

Mark some of your cards for elimination if your audience is getting antsy or if your talk must be shortened owing to some emergency. Things happen—dogs wander in, the electricity fails. Be flexible enough to give up some of your beautifully timed, golden words if people aren't listening.

Reprint any card that is too messy. If you have to cross something out, cross it out completely in heavy black so there is no chance of accidentally reading what you meant to delete. You want to have clean copy in front of you for delivery.

Your final two rehearsals should be from the finished version of your cards, with all the stickers and underlinings in place.

Sample final card. Notice pagination, stickers, wide margins, abbreviations, underlinings, exaggerated punctuation, deep indentation of paragraph, and general legibility.

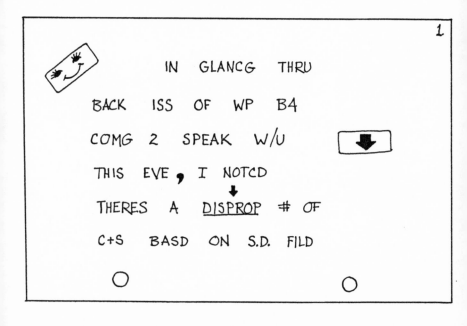

By the way, there are psychological advantages to all this mucking about with cards. The more you handle your material the more comfortable you will feel with it. Physically pushing it around seems to help you feel in control of your talk.

Carrying the cards. A thick rubber band you can trust not to snap will be okay to keep your cards in order until you are ready to use them. The technique we prefer, however, will be apparent to the eagle-eyed reader who spotted the holes punched at the bottom of the sample card.

The neatest, most convenient, most professional-looking and most foolproof way to use cards is to put them in a small notebook. It is worth the few dollars it costs and you can either purchase punched cards to match or punch the holes yourself with a three-hole punch.

When you use a notebook, your cards are never out of order, even if you throw them at somebody. You don't have to practice setting the cards aside after using them because there is only one way they can be turned. Best of all, your notebook sits on the ledge of the podium and this props your notes up high so that you can see them without bringing your head down.

Visual aids. The best advice you will probably ever get about visual aids is "don't use them."

The greatest visual aids consist of erasing the previous speaker's diagram, cleaning up the old coffee cups and saccharin wrappers in the room where you will talk, pulling the curtain so there will be a nice backdrop behind you and closing the Venetian blinds so that the audience members who wear contact lenses will be able to see you through the glare.

Most visual aids are a crutch, a dodge, a distraction. That's why new speakers love them so much. It's true visual aids will take you off center stage, but it's also true that they usually detract from a presentation. Use visual aids only if

you really need them, if they truly add something and if they are very good ones.

Visual aids are helpful if you have to explain a subtle or complicated process that requires listeners to visualize a long series of actions accurately and/or to remember or even memorize them correctly. Sometimes they are very dramatic, such as the classic 1930 profit chart. If you are giving an art lecture, or a scientific paper, you may want to use slides.

To be useful, the visuals must be visible, and the speaker must be thoroughly familiar with them. You really look dippy if you have to stop and think or hunt for the appropriate spot on your chart.

Handouts.   As a general rule, don't give them out until the very end. Audience members will start reading while you are talking. If you want people to follow along with you from item to item, half the audience will probably read page seven when they should be on page five. (The other half of the audience will be whispering about items of interest behind their hands and causing confusion.)

Slides, Transparencies and Film.   A strong visual like slides or film dilutes your personal rapport with the group. It had better be worth it. Structure your presentation so that you aren't constantly having to turn the lights on and off; it takes a while for the eyes to adjust to both dark and light. If an assistant is running the lights, and/or the slide projector changer, be sure she has a copy of your text with her cues marked. Practice working with whatever equipment you use so that you are able to find and to work all the buttons in the dark. You must use slides rather than a flip chart if the group is large. Always keep the back row in mind.

Do not become visibly upset if the technology fails you. By all means ask for help if you need it, but do so in a firm and confident voice. It helps to know the name of the person who can help you. "Alice, the recorder is jammed and we have a frozen image on the monitor." "John, I'm getting a lot of fuzz in this mike." Omit all the "Oh, dears" and hand wringing common to those of us who were socialized to feel edgy at the sight of "equipment." Stay in charge.

Objects.   Keep your "show and tell" items out of sight until you reach the appropriate moment to hold them up. There are shelves built into most podiums—a good place to conceal visual aids. (Members of the audience will keep wondering what the object is if they can see it. Better to have them listen to you.)

If the object is not large enough for everyone to see, you might as well leave it home. If the group is seated close together, you can pass things around without much disruption, but you also run the risk that each individual will tune you out when it's her turn to examine it.

Flip Charts, Blackboards. Uses at briefings include:

An organizational hierarchy
A pie drawing, with percentages represented by slices of the pie
Maps, charts, and other graphics
Large, clear lettering: exact words to be written down by the group (e.g., titles and authors, names of art works and artists, technical terms)

To sum up, to use visual aids effectively use them only when they are necessary and only let them be visible at the exact moment you need them. Don't write on the blackboard until you have to. Keep your flip chart pages covered up or the whole chart stand turned to the wall until it's time to spring it. If you try to write on a flip chart with a marker that is old and faded you will kick yourself for not reminding the liaison ahead of time to get you supplies.

Aids must be simple, clear and visible. Keep your eyes on the audience, not on the visual aid. Point to the item on the chart, then keep talking to the group. Hold up your object, but don't look at it; look at them.

Before you begin your rehearsals make sure that the arrangements with your liaison person are clear.

Suggestions for Common Short Speeches

Announcements. Clear the announcement with the person in charge of the meeting and ask for a specific place on the agenda or a specific time when you can make it. If the meeting is very informal, select a time to jump up when everyone will be willing to hear you. The worst time to make an announcement is just as everyone is leaving the room; their belongings are gathered up, and the noise level is starting to rise. If you want people to make note of a time or date, you will have to announce it when they have their pencils handy.

Your whole voice has to say, "This is interesting." Most announcers take the tone of "I'm saying this because I'm supposed to."

Presenting a gift or award. A gift is usually a symbol of something significant. Stress the reason for giving rather than the gift itself. Don't praise the recipient too lavishly because it will embarrass everyone. Take your mind completely off yourself and put it on the recipient; it is her moment of glory. This is not your show in any way; do not direct attention to yourself. Be careful to hold the gift close to your body until you mean to hand it over. It is very awkward for the recipient if she holds out her hands expecting to take it and you pull it back.

If the occasion is a retirement, remember that this might be a very difficult day for the retiree. Make your tribute warm, understand that this is a life change, a bench mark for her/him that she may regard as depressing. Respect her feelings in every way. If you customarily call everyone "Ms.," or by first name, but the elderly woman who is leaving the company has always been called Mrs. Senior, treat her as she would want to be treated. It is *her* day.

Travel talks. Travel talks are almost always a pain to listen to. The speakers pile detail on detail, and choose the most beautiful adjectives and adverbs to describe what they saw. The problem is too much description and not enough about what happened or how the speaker responded to what she saw. (Also, have you ever noticed that nobody ever says anything *bad* about the scenery?)

Travel speeches lack animation and warmth because the travelers get written out of it. Yes, you want to say what you saw, but please tell us about you, too.

For example: "We saw many children in Mexico—they were everywhere." So what? Did they have flies on them? Did that make you go "Yuck"? Did you kidnap one? Did they make you feel homesick and guilty about your own? Did anything happen? How did it make you feel?

"The scenery was awesome." Who was awed? Were you?

Acceptance Speeches. An audience will forgive you anything if you are sincere. Be simple and brief. If you have received help from others, share the glory with them by emphasizing their role; a solo bow without the cast isn't fair.

Do not look at the prize, look at the person who is presenting it. Don't hold out your hands to take it until it is actually offered to you. As you say your thanks, turn to the audience. Hold the gift in a way that allows everyone else to see it, too. Don't drop the arm holding it to your side.

Now that the arrangements and writing are over, it is time to rehearse and deliver the zippy, earthshaking speech you've prepared.

There is an old story about President Woodrow Wilson that may comfort you at this point. When he was asked how long he would prepare for a ten minute talk, he answered, "Two weeks." For a one-hour speech? "One week." For a two-hour speech? "I'm ready now."

A "professional" speaker, a heavyweight on the lecture circuit, demands complete information on what to expect. You don't want any surprises. Be gently fanatic about all the details with your liaison, and remember that "spontaneity" requires effort. Give yourself all the breaks you can—plenty of time, ample editing, clear cards and rehearsal. Remind yourself that you don't want to be standing eyeball to eyeball with an audience thinking, "Oh, I just wish I had taken the time to do it right."

CHAPTER SIX

Rehearsal and Presentation

You gamble every time you open your mouth. The purpose of rehearsal is to improve the odds that your risk will pay off.

The speaker/audience, platform/auditorium setting is artificial. You will be the same person across the room or from the rostrum as you are at the breakfast table—only more alarmed, and, we hope, better prepared.

Just as an alcoholic doesn't need to lose her compulsion to drink in order to stay sober, you don't have to lose your fear before you can do a good job. You can fake it. Our goal should be to perform so well despite fear that gradually fear dies.

If you rehearse as if you weren't nervous, you will discover that you act pretty much as you practiced when the time comes. Anxiety is always more bearable if you can count on yourself to do an adequate job.

The first time you practice out loud you will either be able to feel the words you have written for yourself or you won't. If you don't feel anything, go back and rewrite.

Rehearsal

We recommend a minimum of six timed, standing up, out loud rehearsals. You must rehearse your presentation out loud; a silent rehearsal is no rehearsal at all. If you're giving a twenty minute speech, this means you will rehearse for at least two hours. A five minute talk requires a half hour of practice. We don't, however, suggest you rehearse all at once. The further you can space your rehearsals the better.

Memorize your opening and closing remarks so that you can say them without using your cue cards. Eighty-five percent eye contact is fine for the middle sections. You do not memorize a whole speech, and you do not read it, either. You memorize the open and the close and familiarize yourself with the rest.

New speakers tend to overrehearse the first third of their presentations. In your anxiety, you may only imagine yourself getting up and saying your opening lines. However, it's much better to remember that you have to say it *all*. Rehearse until the whole speech feels comfortable to you, all the cards look like old friends, and you know the sequence of ideas (but not the language) by heart.

Rehearse the entire speech each time you rehearse. If you fluff lines, or leave something out, keep going and do whatever you would want to do to recover in the "real" speech. Do your talk from the beginning to end each time; don't backtrack to repeat something in a better way if you wouldn't backtrack with the audience listening. To make each rehearsal count, do everything just the way you plan to with the audience, including recovering from mistakes.

Rehearse into a tape recorder. Ear copy is different from eye copy. You are not interested in how the speech looks. How does it sound? Does it make sense? Does it have life? Do you need to vary your pace, your inflection, your pitch? Do you sound monotonous? Does your voice trail off at the end of sentences?

To practice increasing your volume, put the tape recorder at the other end of the room. This will force you to speak up because the mike won't pick up your voice unless you are projecting it.

Rehearse with props. Use a small table for a lectern. Approximate what your speaking setting will be. Visualize your audience by setting up chairs to talk to. Rehearse your visual aids, too.

Rehearse in front of a mirror. Check your body language. If you fidget, or shift your weight from right to left, you will see it and be able to correct it. How much of the time are you looking up from your cards to seek eye contact? If you aren't using a notebook, check to see that you are setting your cards aside when you finish with them, rather than flipping them over.

A "canned," stilted "read" sound doesn't come from too much rehearsal. It comes from being afraid. The more you have rehearsed the easier it will be to make eye contact with the audience. It is genuine contact with the audience that animates a speaker.

Time your rehearsals. If people expect fifteen minutes, they will turn off and tune out after fifteen minutes. It is better to edit a presentation once again to make it short enough to fit the time limit than it is to race through sections of it or to squeeze too many unexplained ideas into the talk. It is better to hear "I could have listened to her all day; her speech wasn't long enough" than "She went on too long."

Rehearse in front of live bodies. You will be less nervous delivering your speech to an audience if, in fact, you have already delivered it to an audience. You will be more relaxed for the real thing if you set up a mock presentation for your preschooler, your landlady, or anyone you can yank off the street to listen. You have to unveil it publicly anyway; lessen your risks by doing it ahead of time.

Ask your guinea pigs for criticism. You may get some good suggestions from objective listeners. If they say there is something they didn't understand, reevaluate.

Since family members and close friends are often the most difficult people to speak in front of, do it! It is a great counterphobic strategy to seek them out. If you can stop feeling self-conscious in front of them you can in front of anyone. Warning: These are the same people who are often the most critical, and you have to *trust your own opinions.* Families are helpful because they know when you're being phony, pompous or stuffy. But beware of family politics, too. Maybe Daddy said it stinks because he's threatened by Mommy doing speeches, period.

If the feedback you get about style is negative, maybe that's because the way you say it isn't exactly the way they would say it. If members of your mock audience don't agree with your talk, hear out why. You can then figure out from their objections how to reinforce your own arguments or be better prepared for possible Question and Answer trouble.

Rehearse with an audio editor. You might ask a friend with good spelling and grammar to correct an article for you. Why not ask someone with a good vocabulary and good English usage to "edit" your speech by listening to you and correcting mispronunciation, malapropisms, clumsy syntax, or incorrect grammar.

Rehearse in your real clothes. Is the outfit you're planning to wear at the presentation comfortable? If the armholes are too tight, you may look rigid and unnatural. You may notice in rehearsal (before it's too late) that your jewelry clanks and distracts, that your hair falls in your eyes and should be pinned back for the speech, that your new skirt has a tag hanging from the back you hadn't noticed before. It's ridiculous to worry about your clothes. Spare yourself by rehearsing them, too.

Rehearse success. No matter how intimidated you may feel, if you force yourself to maintain a positive mental attitude by fantasizing only the good things that can happen, you will be taking the wisdom of thousands of athletes, actors and public speakers to heart (see Chapter Three).

Rehearse Questions and Answers. When you feel adequately prepared for the speech, begin rehearsing your answers to the questions you hope they don't ask (see Chapter Seven).

Delivery

Virtually anyone can acquire speaking skills that are adequate and acceptable for most occasions. Many of us can become very good speakers; it is unfortunate that so few of us do. We would like to change that both because we care about women and because we hate to be bored. Life is too short to waste time either delivering or listening to a dull presentation.

Whether you are a first-timer hoping for adequacy, or an experienced speaker striving for excellence, you can improve your delivery. Here's how.

Take your security blanket. Did you remember to bring a handkerchief, a watch, the names of people who will greet you, directions, your cue cards, visual aids, a mirror, Tampax, Kaopectate, sinus spray, aspirin, paperback books on which to prop your note cards, eyedrops, your glasses, tape recorder, extra nylons?

Establish your territory. Arrange to arrive early. Test the microphone by raising and lowering it to the correct height for your mouth (about six to eight inches away). Don't get too close to the mike. You want to stand far enough away from it so that you still have to project. Ask to have the mike turned on so you can figure out how close you want to be. Don't let them adjust the volume so that you will have to

Lavaliere mikes vary in size. This
is a large one.

speak softly. Remember that when the room is full of bodies
the sound will be deadened and you will have to speak up
even more. If you are using a necklace mike, practice looping
it around your neck and clasping it so you won't get red in
the face and sweaty struggling with the damn thing in front
of the group.

Test the lighting. Take a mirror and view yourself facing
in all directions. If you have light skin and you seem to look
sallow, it may be because the lights have an amber gelatin

placed over them. Request a pink gelatin instead. Do you want more makeup? Less? Is there enough light to see your cards? Is the little light on the podium too harsh? You can either turn it off, or cover it up with Kleenex to soften the glare.

Try to get accustomed to the setting. Feel the podium, walk around it. Practice getting to the spot from which you will be sitting or otherwise waiting. Are you going to have to maneuver stairs, cables for mike and lights? Practice setting your cards down. Are there some last minute changes in the seating that would help you?

The idea is to feel that you are on home territory, that you "own" the furniture, the stage, the equipment. Find out where things are, exactly how they look and feel. Nothing should be strange or unfamiliar—the speech is challenge enough.

Remember that you're "on" before you begin speaking. The audience will form an impression of you before you even open your mouth because of the introducer's words and attitude. The way you act while you are being introduced or *anytime you are visible to the group* influences your reception. Of course, any yawning or head rolls should be done out of sight.

Sit upright and lean a bit forward in your chair. Breathe regularly, with the diaphragmatic breathing exercise in Chapter Two. Concentrate on rhythmic breathing. Allow your shoulders to sag slightly in order to keep relaxed. Your body will be at right angles in your chair, creating an assertive yet relaxed image. Take care not to cross your legs (this cuts off your midsection and you need it for breathing). Don't rotate your ankles around in circles. If you make faces to your friends in the audience, don't expect to be taken seriously when you stand up to speak. Move around from time to time, or you'll get muscle cramps.

Pretend interest in whatever is going on. If you are nervous, you will feel like devoting all of your energy to obsessing about yourself. You already know that the trick to a successful presentation is concentration on your ideas and your audience, so forget about yourself and take (or feign) interest in whatever speeches, rituals, or announcements precede your talk. A speaker with her nose in her own notes ignoring the group's cherished anthem is a speaker who is just asking for trouble.

Psych yourself. Choose to control what goes on in your mind while you wait to be called on. Try repeating one or more of the phrases suggested below to mesmerize yourself. Say them until you believe them. Even if you don't believe them (yet), at least keep your brain busy with practical and positive language. Don't allow time or room for thoughts that are scary ("I'll never remember...") or negative ("I can't go through with this"). Thinking negative thoughts takes as much energy as thinking helpful ones.

Heighten your impulse to communicate by repeating:

"I want them to understand this. I think I can do it."

"I'm glad to be here. I'm *glad* to be here."

"I know what I'm talking about, and I feel prepared."

"This will be okay. They look nice."

Remember that you *want* to feel a bit nervous, up, energized; your psych lines are to keep you from letting the good nerves turn to jitters.

Last Minute Routine

Put all your toys away. You want to take only a handkerchief, your notes and your watch with you to the podium. If you have a pencil in your hand when you are called on, the chances are that you will take it with you to the podium and play with it throughout your speech.

Alternate between glancing at your opening lines (so they will be on the tip of your tongue), and thinking through your psych thoughts. Every now and then, imagine the sequence of actions you plan to go through when your name is called (see below).

You're On!

It's time to enjoy yourself, or fake it. Vow to give it your best shot. If you have written a miserable speech, try to pull it out with a good delivery. It is time to *do the best you can with what you've got*, because right now it's all you've got. Go!

Walk briskly to the platform. Do not drag or shuffle your feet; a positive, yet unhurried stride suggests alertness and readiness. If you approach the podium as though it were a guillotine (or rush away from it when your talk is over) you undermine yourself.

Take your time before you begin. Settle your cards in a comfortable position, find a stance that suits you, adjust the mike if you need to, let your arms and hands fall at your sides, or rest lightly at the lectern.

Face the house for about a count of six (or until they settle down), looking them over as if to size up the situation and make sure they're listening. When you pause you project a quiet authority and firm confidence.

Begin at a low pitch, with adequate volume. Your face should register good news and interest, and your body should be steady and under control. Your first few sentences may be shaky if you are very nervous. Your legs might shake, your stomach may clench. The beginning is usually the worst time for a speaker's particular symptom (maybe you will experience them all!). Don't worry about this. The last thing you should punish yourself for is nerves. You will relax as you go along. Don't be nervous about being nervous. By the time you've reached your conclusion you will feel better.

If this is your first "speech" you may find after it is all over that you went into a trancelike state, and you can hardly remember what happened. The speech goes by like a blur, and it's over before you're fully conscious again. If your speech is tightly organized, lucidly argued and well re-hearsed, you will probably deliver it on "automatic pilot" just as you delivered it during rehearsal. People will listen, and it will be a success. If you have confidence in what you are about to say, your subconscious will feel okay about the delivery. We put a great deal of emphasis on preparing well for a presentation because even the worst speaker cannot entirely kill a good, well-rehearsed speech. Of course, an excellent speaker may successfully pull off a virtuoso performance of a shallow speech, too.

If your reaction to the unfamiliarity of giving a talk (report, announcement, whatever) is going into a trance, you are likely, once it is over, to be tempted to demonstrate great signs of relief. Do not throw away your hard work by sighing, giggling with a friend. Just don't. Save the story about how "it all went by so fast I didn't even know it was happening" for later.

Posture

The best posture allows for freedom of activity. People sense your confidence, feelings of security, self-assurance, courage and strength from your bodily manner just as they do from your words.

Poise *is* efficient bodily behavior that fits the communicative situation. The opposite of poise is random, needless, repetitious or awkward movement.

Movement If You Are Using a Mike

If you have a necklace mike you have lots of freedom of movement. Most mikes, however, are freestanding or attached to a podium. You don't want to move "off mike" so your movements are quite restricted. Lean forward on the podium to establish intimacy, or for dramatic effect. You can do this once or twice to make a point without looking as though you're so weary you have to lean on the rostrum for support.

Don't keep looking at the mike. It won't move. It won't

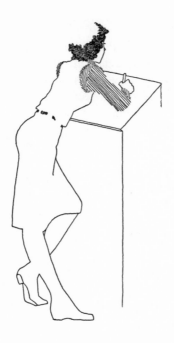

Stand on both feet.

bite. The ear-splitting electronic whine, that screeching feedback sound you love to hate, sometimes comes from the speaker standing too closely to the mike.

Movement If You Are Not Using a Mike

Your goal is purposeful movement, not nervous energy that results in random, distracting movements. If in everyday life you have been practicing substituting relaxed but controlled movements of your hands, arms and feet for random, jerky flailings, then you are bound to appear more poised during your speech. If you don't have good habits yet, pay attention to the body language stickers on your cards.

Generally, keep your eyes on the audience when you move, and don't move suddenly. Initiate a movement, such as stepping three paces to the left, in a lazy fashion and end it lazily. Wait a while before returning back to the right. Move to the sides at an angle.

Move away from the lectern and toward the audience to emphasize major points. You can also move from one side of the rostrum to the other as you make transitions from one subject to another. Do not pace. The audience will start counting your steps.

Gestures

Do not invent gestures or plan them. They should be genuine and spontaneous, resulting from normal freedom of action and the absence of nervous movement. Meaningful gestures are controlled, but not wooden or militarily stiff. A "gesture" is not fluffing your hair, rubbing your knuckles, twisting your ring or smoothing your dress. These are meaningless fidgets resulting from lack of control.

Cards

If you have no podium, hold your cards away from your body and higher than your waist. You don't want to obscure your face, but you want to be able to drop your eyes to the cards, not your whole head.

Do not apologize for reading or attempt to conceal your notes. If you are well rehearsed you should have no trouble finding your place unerringly unless you're holding the cards so awkwardly that you can't see them very well.

If you are not using a notebook, you should set each card to the side as you finish with it. Do not flip cards over because this is obtrusive and may obscure your face. Of course, if you have no lectern you are forced to place used cards behind the stack. If you do have a lectern, do not try to put each card behind the stack of cards left to read because you might accidentally slip one back into the stack and find yourself staring at it again. Brush your cards to the side. When you have finished speaking you will need a few extra seconds to stack them together neatly. Do not briskly gather your notes together and whack them on something to bring the edges in line. This is officious.

Face

For the first few minutes you can limit your eye contact to those faces that seem the most sympathetic and responsive, but after that you have to find out who is with you and who isn't and why. People's faces will tell you that they are puzzled, or they can't hear, or that you've gone flat.

Audiences take on the emotions of the speaker. If your face registers joy, they will begin to feel it, too. If you look unpleasant or fearful the audience will absorb it and return it. Why not trigger love by looking at them as though you believe life isn't *that* grim.

Remember that your expression should be appropriate to your words. The incongruity of a pleasant smile nullifies the effect of a serious argument. If you are talking about drug addiction or making a demand, don't smile. Don't smile if you are afraid your face will crack and fall off. An interested, enthusiastic expression is okay, too.

Overdo It

Exaggeration in print looks suspicious. In a speech, it makes a good impression. Speech delivery settings flatten you out. Don't be afraid of strong emphasis or drama on a stage, in a TV studio or in front of a classroom. The overstating you feel you are doing is probably coming across as understated and bland. Your interest in your subject must be avid, and *show*.

Don't Be Afraid of Silences

If you mess up, shut up until you've recovered. Do not use fillers (ums, deep breaths, waving your hands, muttering, making things up as you go along). It is better to pause and be quiet, to make the audience wait, than to babble. Unskilled speakers usually read too quickly. Pause for effect whenever your cue cards say to.

Don't Be Afraid of Noises

People drop things. People cough. People change their seats.

Pretend to Digress

The audience does not want to be read to; they want "talk." Act as though you are departing from your script from time to time (to tell a secret, to say something that just popped into your head), even though you aren't. Surely you know some sections of the talk well enough by now to do them eyes up and in an "impromptu" manner.

Exit

Your body language as well as your words will let the audience know you have finished. Give them a nod of the head or a quick step back from the mike. Gather your cards calmly, looking up to acknowledge the applause, and leave the stage/podium/front of the room the way you arrived—briskly, and firmly. You are "on" until you are out of sight completely (meaning back at home, not just back to your chair). If you roll your eyes, shrug your shoulders, sigh, or in any way say "God, I'm glad *that's* over" or "Oh, hell, did

I ever screw *that* one up," you will wreck the effect of the speech. You "take back" everything you said by acting relieved or behaving as though you have just play-acted the adult giving a talk, and now it's time to resume being a little girl. You may *feel* that way, but do the audience the courtesy of keeping it to yourself. From beginning to end, the *very* end, communicate what you planned, not what feelings you may be trying to overcome.

Without sounding like Pollyannas may we suggest that there is almost always something to be proud of in any speech. Even after the presentation is over you should be good to yourself. Smile if it's appropriate and look pleased with yourself. It may not have been the best performance ever but it was the best you could do that day under those circumstances. So be proud.

Afterwards—Critiquing Your Own Speech

A practical test of how your speech went is to ask whether the audience responded by talking about what you said. Were there questions, objections or arguments in the days and weeks following your talk? Did you stimulate discussion? No matter whether you were dazzling or dull, view your performance objectively. Regret is wasteful.

To Improve

Remember that all speech is public speaking. Speak often. The more you assert yourself in every speaking situation the easier it will become. In fact, you may become addicted to it as we have. The power to communicate, to reach out and share with an audience, to influence other people even briefly is heady stuff. It increases your confidence and that in turn increases your ability—the very antithesis of the self-defeating vicious circle that has caught women up for years. It may not seem revolutionary, when your cooperative nursery school asks you to do an orientation session for new parents, or when your boss asks you to present a report at the next staff meeting, or your church asks you to make an appeal for funds, but it is, it is.

> We can do anything we want
> if we stick to it long enough.
> HELEN KELLER

CHAPTER SEVEN

Questions and Answers

Even if you think your speech went smoothly and you feel proud of your performance, you will probably feel let down if the question and answer period is listless. A good speaker wants to parry questions, the tougher the better, from the audience.

As we have been insisting all along, a good speech has the air of a dialogue. During the question period the feedback you have been getting throughout your speech from facial expressions, body language and your intuition about the audience becomes concrete verbal response. Ideally, it is time to share the responsibility that has been yours alone up to now.

Questions can be full of peril. This is not the time to lose control or forget what you are there to do, namely, persuade the audience to accept the information you have or the point of view you wish to promote.

Quite often inexperienced speakers visibly relax and become more animated and "real" after the speech itself is over. It is clear they feel relieved. This is more like it, they seem to be thinking, this is the way people really talk to each other. Unfortunately, a radical change in manner may undermine what has gone before. It gives the impression that the speaker was putting on an act. If you assume a different personality for Q & A, either your speech was too stiff or your Q & A manner is too "I take it all back; I'm just a kid." A marked change may be a danger signal that the speaker doesn't recognize that she is still the speaker, still the focus of attention, still on. The Question and Answer period *counts*.

And what if there are no questions at all? We assume that when a subject catches a person's interest, she will want to know more. The tradition of question and answer periods springs from this assumption. It can be a real blow to discover that we haven't sparked a response from the audience.

To insure success in a question and answer period, you must make sure that there will be questions. You must also understand the dynamics of this speaking situation so that you will parry the questions effectively.

Make Sure There Are Questions

Pros never go anywhere to speak to anyone without seeding the audience. Talk show hosts on radio and television, politicians and public speakers of all kinds can count on getting good questions because they put them there. They give some friendly person in the audience a question or two to ask whenever things seem to lag or if the audience is shy about beginning. Don't feel hesitant about setting someone up to ask you questions. Anyone will do, a friend or neighbor, or if you are in a completely strange place you can call on your well-worn liaison person. What is the question you would most like to be asked, the question that would really start the ball rolling, the question for which you have a brilliant reply? Plant it.

If there is still a lull after your planted questions, you can even ask yourself questions: "Many of the women I talk to seem especially concerned about being drafted for combat duty..." or, "Last week a man in my neighborhood said, 'If you don't want to be treated like a lady, then...'" This ploy, let's face it, has to be managed with great confidence and even then is a bit phony. It is a stopgap measure for hard times. Make sure the questions you ask yourself are very hard and nasty ones, otherwise you'll look even phonier. If you find yourself using this technique a lot, go back to the beginning of this book and start over. You are doing something wrong. An audience should have questions after the ice has been broken, and if they don't you haven't reached them.

Another Q & A trick is to laugh, say "You mean nobody here wants to know about... (insert the worst, most hostile, embarrassing, hardest question you can think of)?" In the general laughter and murmuring that follows, one person is bound to call out "Yeah, I do" or "Sure, tell us." Pounce on that person and treat your answer as though it had come from her, from the floor. In timid audiences (high school groups come to mind) nobody wants to go first. If you can make it seem as though somebody asked a question, others may want to participate.

There are occasionally audiences so hostile, inarticulate or frightened that nobody could wrench a response from them. The moment to find out that you have encountered one of these rare audiences is not during the question and answer period (see Chapter Four). Prepare for them in advance by asking your liaison, "Do they usually ask a lot of questions? How have they responded to speakers like me in the past?" If your liaison suggests that this audience has never been coaxed into jumping up and down with eager questions, you can arrange to have written, and therefore anonymous, questions from them turned in to the liaison ahead of time. This is an emergency technique. Use it only when you have strong evidence that nobody is likely to ask the things they really have on their minds for fear of seeming ignorant, for fear of being identified with an unpopular concept, or for fear of assuming the role of "speaker" long enough to ask a question in front of the whole group. If the liaison agrees, ask her to collect scraps of paper with the questions on them. Go early to choose the ones you want to address yourself to if and when the group balks at your other question-eliciting techniques.

You, of course, have done your best to write and deliver a speech that is likely to provoke a response from this particular group, and if you don't stir them you can say, "oh, well" and not go home and kick the cat.

These difficult audiences, thank goodness, are few and far between. So we will repeat: If you are failing to get questions time after time you need to rethink your approach. You have not been effective. Do not despair. Any audience response is feedback and the purpose of feedback is to help you to make corrections. No response at all is feedback of a particularly dramatic and unpleasant sort; however, be objective: figure out what went wrong and fix it.

People Will Want to Argue with You

You will never get the following question: "Everything you said was absolutely compelling and my only question is, where do I sign up?" What you will get is a lot of arguments. It is human nature to be skeptical and our natural tendency has been reinforced further through years of schooling. Teacher was always proud when you argued and asked hard, so-called "good" questions because it meant you were paying attention and were interested. It still does. Listen to radio talk shows, or the people at meetings, and especially listen to other speakers' talks. Almost all questions fall into the general category of arguing. There are attempts to show the speaker is wrong by citing new evidence, arguing with the evidence she has used, pointing out inconsistencies, telling long stories about an exception to a generalization she has made and lots of others. This is all benign and never hurt anyone. A smart woman like you with all her facts straight can handle these kinds of questions easily. Expect to get an argument; certainly don't be defensive about it.

We would also include under the general heading of "benign questions" such things as simple requests for additional information, fuller explanation of one of your points and documentation of your evidence. The people who make these requests may or may not agree with you, and you may or may not have the answer or wish to answer, but these are all friendly questions. (No matter how upset it makes you to be asked for documentation for a statistic that you just made up in the heat of the moment, the question is still fair; you shouldn't make up statistics . . . now you're stuck.)

Answering Friendly Questions

Answering a question is a short impromptu speech. The basics are the same whether you are answering questions from behind a podium, during a job interview, at a press conference or while talking about sex with a five-year-old. As we suggest in Chapter Eight, relax, maintain your poise and edit to a point. Relaxation comes from the firm conviction that you know more about your subject than your audience does; that is why you are the speaker. It also comes from having prepared a list of the questions you are most likely to get and writing out answers to them for rehearsal. If you have any lingering doubts, get rid of them. You know more and you care and you are completely prepared. There may be questions that you can't answer from time to time, but there won't be many.

Maintain eye contact with the whole audience and not just with the person who has asked the question. Unless the question is very simple, paraphrase it before answering so that you are sure you are answering to the point. It is also a good idea to repeat the question because not everyone in the audience may have heard it. For example:

Q: "Are you in favor of prostitution?"

Your Paraphrase: "I think you are asking me whether I favor decriminalization of prostitution, that is removing the legal penalties for practicing it. Is that right?"

Q: "Yes."

A: "Because blah blah blah, and because blah, yes I do."

Remember to be brief. Think first of your conclusion, support it with one or two reasons, state it and shut up. Be funny if you can but never score off nice people. That means that no matter how witty you are and no matter how dumb the question or how perfect an opening it gives you, you will not say anything that makes your questioner feel stupid or foolish and lets the audience laugh at her. Remember, you have the power, you are the expert and you are also more experienced at talking in public than most of your audience. When you are nervous and unsure of yourself it is easy to dismiss how much power you have standing there behind the podium, but don't forget it and don't misuse it. We repeat, never make a nice person's question the springboard for a joke on that person.

Be succinct. (You notice this is not the first time we have urged this.) Not everyone in your audience will want to hear the answer to this question and furthermore they have just listened to you talk for twenty minutes and they want a chance to talk, too. Long-winded answers are boring, fail to persuade and scare the audience into thinking you are about to begin your speech all over again. They may have a plane to catch.

How Not to Answer a Friendly Question

There may be sincere and well-meant questions that you either cannot or do not wish to answer. If you do not know an answer, don't guess. If you are well prepared you can usually steer the questioner toward an appropriate resource even if you don't know all the facts by heart. For example:

"I don't have the statistics on Chicana women who are the heads of their households but you can find them in the Women's Bureau of the Department of Labor Handbook on Women Workers."

or

"I don't know the exact number of returnees to abortion clinics but certainly the women's health collective, or the NOW Task Force on Abortion, would know."

It is a good idea to announce the limits of your area of competence before and during a question and answer period. If you have come to talk about lesbianism, you do not want to answer questions concerning career opportunities for the mature woman, and you don't have to no matter how relevant the question may appear to your questioner. If it is possible to pave the way for an answer that you do want to give, then do so. The beauty of vague or open-ended questions is that you can answer as you wish, make your own point. Otherwise, just say, "That's an interesting question and one I'd love to discuss, but I'm not qualified to give you solid information on it." Or, "That's a good question, but it isn't what we are talking about right now; I'd prefer to reserve this time for questions about _____."

There are also dumb and irrelevant questions that you do know the answer to but don't want to waste your time with. This happens frequently with reporters and interviewers in the media who don't know what to ask because they haven't done their homework (see Chapter Eleven). Ilka Chase once said ". . . if once in a lifetime you find yourself up against a stupid group, don't let them know that you think so. That stupid they are not." This is excellent advice.

There are also dumb questions that are not even questions but just somebody in the audience making his own speech. The trick to dealing with these is to steer the asker toward a question you do want to answer. For example:

Q: "I have this elderly woman friend who gardens a lot and she was out in her garden the other day and got so sunburned that we're really concerned about her. Don't you think that older people should wear hats?"

A: "Probably. I think that gardening is a good example of the kind of work women who have been in the home for many years ignore when they start the career counseling process. When asked what we like to do, many of us fail to include gardening, sports or civic activities that may tell a great deal about what we like and what we're good at."

If the questioner in this case has tried to go on and on about taking his friend to the hospital and about the callous doctor and how hard it was to find a parking place and so forth, you must interrupt him. "Will you state your question, please?" Do not allow members of the audience to make speeches. It is bad enough when they are boring and irrelevant or inaudible, but it becomes downright dangerous when such speeches are unfriendly.

There are also friendly questions that you don't want to answer because it would take too long. Just say so. Indicate briefly the direction your answer would take and invite the person to stay after the speech to discuss the matter with you, and then move on. We repeat, don't make a new speech. Be brief. Let your people go.

Hostile Questions, Hostile Audiences

A casual opponent is a person who has heard more arguments against your opinion than for it, and asks for information in a challenging, though not closed-minded way. Her questions, however difficult, still fall within the outside limits of rational and "friendly" ("I believe you mean what you say, but I'm not convinced. Who else says so? Give me some more examples"). Audiences that strongly disagree with you may still be friendly.

Then there are hostile audiences and hostile questions. It's important to draw this distinction because if you are so nervous and defensive (many of us are) that any reaction short of total affection makes you furious and tearful then your first encounter with a *really* hostile audience will probably kill you and we wouldn't want to be responsible for that. Try to head into Q & A with a few reminders to yourself that although you may be hungry for approval and love, you will survive if you don't get it here.

It is important to make sure you do not mistake reasonable disagreement for malignant attack. The distinction is not always immediately clear because people are not usually completely open about hating you. In fact, they may not even realize for a while they do hate you. We think it is safe to say that certain kinds of questions are inherently hostile. Any question based on a stereotype about your sex, race, religion or age is probably not going to lead to fruitful dialogue. (For example, alcoholic Indian questions, money-grubbing Jew questions, dumb broad questions, impotent old man questions and a zillion others.) You will notice that there are a great many stereotypes about a great many kinds of people; women aren't the only ones who suffer. You should notice this so you won't become bitter and twisted before you have given your third speech. Having said that, let's go on to talk about what happens to us as women specifically.

Ways of thinking and talking about women that feminists have pinpointed as insulting are still second nature and taken for granted in a lot of places. A man who would no longer dare call a Native American "Chief" in a jocular friendly way or a Black man "boy" will still refer to all women as "dear" and think nothing of it. There are still plenty of places where a woman who doesn't choose to have children, or who doesn't like taking care of her children, or who thinks children are tiresome, is considered an unnatural monster. The problem is that an audience may have a lot of unconscious stereotyped notions about you that are hostile in and of themselves; on top of that they will hate you for not accepting their stereotypes.

For example:

> Q: "But look, sweetheart, if we cut back ten percent on the marketing budget . . ."
>
> A: "Mr. Jones, it makes me feel uncomfortable to be called 'sweetheart.' Please stop."
>
> Q: "Oh, for crissakes, you women are driving me crazy with this shit. What's the matter with you, blah, blah."

You see how very angry it makes Mr. Jones when you object to his attempt to discredit you?

As we have noted, it is "unfeminine" to stand behind a podium and make a speech. A woman behaving in any new or different way makes some people angry. This may surprise you if your speech itself is completely uncontroversial. It isn't your speech, it's your powerful delivery that upsets them. Alas, the better a job you do, the more uneasy you make some people.

Questions about your personal life are almost always hostile unless your personal life has been your topic or the audience is very young. Young people have a great curiosity about how grown-ups live, eat, sleep (and with whom), got their jobs and so forth. Young people try to find role models and it's probably all right for them to ask, but it's not anyone else's business.

You can say "I would prefer not to answer that question," and go on to the next one. You do not have to defend your preference or explain it. Personal questions are improper, and the answers to them can always be used against you (what does she know, she's so young, so old).

Trick questions are always hostile. If they liked you why would they want to trick you? Trick questions are questions that show you to be a dangerous fool or an evil corrupt person no matter how you answer them. The point of the question is buried in such a way that you may not catch it at first. For example:

> Q: "A woman like you probably hasn't had any trouble, but don't you find that most women are too emotional for high-powered positions?"

No matter how you explain stereotypes about women and emotion, unless you confront the buried attack you have been had. The questioner has planted in the mind of the rest of the audience the notion that you are different, possibly unnatural, and therefore, probably a dangerous person. A corollary of this approach is to ask you questions that gradually get you to think and say "Women...they are misunderstood." If you separate yourself from womankind then the audience can easily apply all their "bad unnatural woman" stereotypes to everything you say. You collude in your own downfall by agreeing implicitly that you are different from other women.

Another example of a trick question is one with a false assumption or two hidden in it. For example:

Q: In the animal kingdom the male is always dominant but you seem to think that humans, who are, after all, animals, can go against nature without harm.

Q: Since women are absent from work more than men, doesn't it make sense to make sure a woman is reliable before giving her a promotion?

Q: If women want to dump their kids in some day-care center and run off to work, it's okay with me, but I want to know who is going to take care of the guys put out of jobs?

The hardest part of formulating a response is trying to decide whether the buried false assumption is a trick in itself. Is it an attempt to sidetrack you into an argument that is silly and irrelevant? We have had animal kingdom discussions up to here and don't really want to do it again, but on the other hand if the entire audience really believes that the male is dominant, then maybe...and so on. You have to steer a fine course between tiresome red herring discussions without allowing too many false premises and misconceptions to go by.

Last but not least are insults so sugarcoated that they are hard to locate at all. The Smile and Screw school of question-posing includes all the friendly condescending help you get from people whose (covert) point is that you couldn't possibly know what you are talking about because you are female.

> "If all you lovely young ladies would take into account the statistics on . . ."

> "I think you did a terrific job with your little speech just now and I . . ."

> "You couldn't be expected to know this, but . . ."

Any implication that what you think and say is stupid, uninformed or trivial should be confronted directly. Since each woman has a different style, the "right" comeback for one woman won't work for another. For example, the speaker could interrupt: "What do you mean, 'little' speech? I'll have you know that was a jumbo speech. Now what is your little question?" in a humorous fashion that would make her point without making an enemy. The same approach will fall flat—or insult—if it is not consistent with the speaker's personality.

Answering a Hostile Question

The first step in dealing with a hostile audience is one you should take before even leaving the house. As we pointed out in Chapter Four, it is critical that you have background information on your audience before you go to speak. If you are sure that the audience is going to disagree with you, then you can prepare yourself psychologically. The object is not to work yourself up into a defensive rage; in fact, it is just the reverse. Before you begin, try to understand the opinions and feelings of the people who are going to disagree. You are going to set the tone of this "meeting of the minds" so you must be objective, friendly and reasonable yourself or all is lost. That is very hard especially in the heat of discussion after people have been attacking you. It helps to psych yourself ahead of time. Repeat one hundred times, "They are uninformed and don't understand; they're frightened; they hate what I stand for, not me . . . ," and so forth. Most of us think of ourselves as nice people, very ordinary conventional folks who just happen to be involved in ozone box therapy and are going to chat about it to some nice people from the American Psychoanalytical Society. We have a tendency to be surprised and injured when we are attacked as dangerous radical crazies because, to us, our position seems eminently reasonable. If it didn't we wouldn't hold it. The point is, don't be surprised when people hate you, and want to destroy your credibility and ego. It's a vale of tears, bubeleh. You may think you are psychologically prepared, but unless you have encountered a hostile audience before you probably aren't. Don't worry if you aren't sharp and witty and brilliant in your first encounter. Nobody is. Most of us are really upset and hurt. You get used to it, and before you know it you are handling it like a pro. You are not likely to convert a prejudiced audience so sometimes the best you can hope for in writing and delivering your speech is to keep things on a rational friendly level and take care not to offend with a careless remark.

It is easy for us, of course, veterans of many such battles, to blithely tell you to relax and not worry. The truth is that only experience makes it easier. Experience thickens the hide and builds your confidence and also helps you to realize that the worst that can happen isn't much. So go out and get experience. Start with small, friendly groups if you can and work up. There are a million audiences and you can pretty much judge how hostile they are likely to be. Trim your speaking engagements to how strong you think you have become. If you have never given a speech before and cry easily, don't start by delivering a presentation advocating twenty-four-hour-a-day child care on demand (to be paid for with the money we save by cutting the defense budget in half) to the American Legion Post 876 of Smalltown, Indiana.

Now for the specifics.

Paraphrase. When the audience is hostile it becomes even more important to understand exactly what they are asking you. While it is fine to ask "What do you mean?" or "Do you mean *x?*" (paraphrase the question) as a clarification device, don't do it when you know perfectly well what awful things the questioner is asking/saying. Then your "What do you mean?" becomes nonassertive avoidance (based on the shaky hope that the questioner will hang himself by elaborating). It works better to confront the situation and say what you think.

Try saying "I can't answer your whole question, but if part of what you would like to know is _____, my answer is _____." Or, "If you mean by '_____,' '_____,' " then my answer is '_____.'"

Feel free to say "Let me think a moment," before you plunge into dangerous territory. Divide up questions, especially those based on several misconceptions. Change the subject if you must: "I don't believe we have enough time for me to comment on *x*, but I would like to say something about *y*, which is related."

Be honest. This cannot be stressed too strongly. An audience senses when you are lying or dodging an issue or fudging an answer and they will not like you any better for doing it. They hate you anyway, remember, so you might as well aim for respect. For example, if someone asks you why you want to work instead of taking care of your children and you launch into a long lyrical description of how much you love your children and how you are working because you think it's better for them, don't expect to be believed. Your work in fact may be good for your children, but we both know that's not why you work and so does the audience.

If someone in the audience points out that you have made an error of fact, stand tall and say, "You are correct, and I was incorrect."

Do not theorize, speculate or talk abstractly. Stick as closely as you can to your own experience, your own feelings or well-documented evidence. Offer as little room for argument as possible. Unless you want to have a shouting, shoving brouhaha, don't bring up speculative abstract issues. There may be a few who will argue with you if you say "I am deeply religious." There are many who will argue if you say "Deep religious feelings are all that distinguish human beings from other animals." Similarly, it is hard to argue with the fact that the Department of Labor says that 40 percent of the work force is female and this figure is up from 29 percent in 1950. It is easy to argue violently with statements like, "It won't be long before all women work their whole lives just like men."

Avoid falling into an exclusive dialogue with one nasty person. Listen attentively to the question, but while you are answering it, maintain eye contact with the audience as a whole. Don't answer more than one question from a person who doesn't like you or your answers.

Prevent speeches from the audience. A questioner should be allowed thirty seconds or so to fully develop a question if it is complicated, but not allowed to make a speech. Interrupt to ask what the question is.

Don't score off questioners. Most of the time a very agitated hostile question comes from someone who represents the fears and concerns of the whole audience. You will not win friends by using your superior wit to destroy this person. Even the most dismal boor deserves your courtesy because you have the advantage. You are the speaker, you are the powerful authority. He is speaking from the floor, without introduction or formal legitimation. If you use a put-down, the audience will feel sympathy for your victim and not for you. The only time this isn't true is when one individual monopolizes the Q & A and makes everyone mad. When you manage to shut the speaker up, the audience will be grateful. The best strategy is to call on other questioners and say, "I'd like to hear from some of the rest of you."

Do not try to shout down hecklers. There is no clever trick to dealing with serious heckling. Don't even try to deal with it. You are obligated because you have taken the platform to put up with an audience's ignorance and their threat level, which they may express in the form of hostility, but you owe no one an apology for refusing to accept abuse. Shouting back won't help, witty remarks won't be heard and people who might be reasoned with about the injustice of heckling won't be the ones who are doing it. Make a calm announcement to the effect that you cannot and will not speak under the circumstances and leave. Period. The liaison person, organizational chairperson, program director or whoever can appeal to the crowd to behave themselves; that is not your job. If the heckling is just getting started and is sporadic you can say that you plan to stop speaking unless the heckling stops, but it probably won't work. Don't worry if this happens. People who refuse to allow another to speak because they disagree with her position are beneath contempt. Don't waste your time being concerned.

Wrapping Up a Question and Answer Period

As we pointed out in Chapter Five, a weak conclusion can ruin a perfectly good talk. Remember that your question and answer period is part of your speech and bring it to a strong conclusion. Women have been brought up to be polite and ladylike (as we have said a hundred times now) and will often go on bravely answering questions long beyond the time to call a halt simply because there are still people asking and it seems rude to cut them off. You must stop when the end has come and stop decisively. How do you know when?

Most speaking engagements run about forty minutes, with twenty minutes or so for the speech and twenty minutes for Q & A. Unless you are in a workshop or very informal fireside chat where lengthy discussion is appropriate, twenty minutes is plenty of time for Q & A, so after twenty minutes, STOP.

At the risk of belaboring the obvious, the best time to stop is before the audience runs out of questions. It makes you look bad to say, after waiting hopefully, "Well, if there aren't any more questions, I guess I'll step down...." Wistfulness is not the effect we are striving for. As soon as the questions stop coming thick and fast (three or four people with their hands up at once) it's time to quit. Don't beg or look disappointed. Always leave while people still want a little more.

Alert the audience that you have only a few moments left. Don't say "I can take one more question"; what if the next question is terrible? If possible, call the halt just after you have answered brilliantly and not after you've been forced to hedge or say you don't know. Remember, this is the conclusion of your speech. Make it count.

Leave time for private questions. There will be members of every audience who prefer to ask their questions in private after the speech. Say something like "I'm afraid we're going to have to stop . . . it was a pleasure talking with you." Smile, acknowledge the applause, put your papers and notes together and step away. Then, while you pause to be thanked by the liaison person, let your motions be slow and relaxed so those who wish to approach you will feel that you are accessible. Warning: sometimes a person who comes up afterwards will be a bore who will want to monopolize you for another hour or two recounting their life's story. Don't feel obliged to listen beyond a brief question or two. Heart to hearts are appropriate only if you feel like having one, which you probably won't, having just spent an intense hour on stage. Cut the person off and turn to someone else. If there isn't anyone else just say that you must go, and go.

CHAPTER EIGHT

An Introduction Is a Speech

> "Mommy, this is Jamey.
> He eats frogs."

Social Introductions

The purpose of a social introduction is to tell people enough about each other so they can begin a conversation. Etiquette manuals advise us to say the name of the "senior" person first. ("Madame President, this is Jane Elioseff. Ms. Elioseff, may I present our President, Kathy Griffin.") The "senior" person is defined as the one who is older, of higher rank, or, when women and men are being introduced, the woman is to be given the courtesy of being named first.

We think these conventions are ageist, sexist, classist and deserving of swift death. Similarly, we feel uncomfortable with introductions that dwell on the individual's rank, status or "importance" in male institutions. Try to describe yourself and others in ways that don't promote categories of "who matters and who doesn't" or "the somebodies and the nobodies." An egalitarian introduction focuses on information two unique individuals might like to share with each other, without emphasizing a hierarchy of authority or power between them. Most of us feel more at ease when we hear what we have in common with someone we are meeting for the first time.

If you don't know how to introduce someone, ask, "What shall I say about you?" and then give her plenty of time to think of her answer.

If you don't care for the way a colleague introduces you to new coworkers or if you are being introduced by your party host in language you don't like, it is your responsibility to suggest a two-sentence self-description she or he can use.

Shaking Hands

Extend your hand automatically to *anyone* to whom you are being introduced or to anyone to whom you introduce yourself, regardless of age, sex or circumstances. (Shake hands with children, with people on the street, at casual gatherings and during business interviews.) You go first; if you take the initiative the other person won't have to do an agitated two-step wondering whether a handshake is appropriate. A firm, brief handclasp while looking into the eyes (not down at the hands) of the other person establishes you as someone who wishes to be friendly *and* to be taken seriously.

Introducing Yourself—Your Verbal Résumé

Most of us would rather not talk at all than have to introduce ourselves to strangers, especially to an audience of them. Furthermore, we know so much about ourselves that it's difficult to sum ourselves up with a few labels.

However, when you must introduce yourself, it is comforting to have a simple, brief résumé. An effective thumbnail sketch of who you are is tough to invent on the spot, so figure out what to say in advance. Who are you?

You will be glad you put in the energy, thought and practice every time you go into a job interview, walk up to a new face at a party or go unintroduced before an audience if you have decided ahead of time how to describe yourself.

A verbal résumé should include, at the barest minimum, your name and your reason for introducing yourself into the situation. For example:

> "Hi, I'm Ellen Wade. I live in the green house on the corner and I confess I've been watching you move in all afternoon. I just stopped by to say hello and welcome. I've lived around here for years, so I can probably answer questions you might have."

When a job interviewer says "Tell me a little something about yourself," perhaps your answer will concern something you can say about yourself today you couldn't have said five years ago. Depending on the circumstances, you may want to explain your immediate goals or long-range objectives in your career development. Perhaps you want to introduce yourself in terms of what motivates you, or what you want to be able to say you have accomplished when you retire.

In describing yourself to an audience, the identity or credentials you select may concern what you do for a living or your major interests, but whatever you choose should be relevant to the group.

Never say, "I'm Mrs. Lewis" or "Ms. Lewis" or "Miss Lewis." Always say "I'm Louise Lewis." It is rude to call yourself by your title. If people need to know that you are a doctor or that you prefer to keep the relationship on a courtesy title basis, then signal this in other ways. On the telephone, for instance, you can say, "I'm Louise Lewis. Please call me Lou. What do you like to be called?" In the unlikely event that the answer is "Mr. Swine," it is wise quickly to add, "Ah, then please call me Ms. (Mrs., Miss, Dr.) Lewis."

If you know the other person's name, the introduction can go like this: "Hi, this is Louise Lewis, Mr. Allen." If Mr. Allen calls you Louise after you addressed him by his surname, you have two choices. If you agreed to make the relationship informal, as he has indicated he wants to do, then begin at once to use his first name. If you don't know it, ask. If you prefer to keep the conversation formal and that is what you meant to indicate when you called him by his last name, make your intention even clearer by saying at once, "Perhaps you didn't hear my surname. I'm Ms. Lewis, Mr. Allen."

Titles among adults should be reciprocal. Do not allow anyone to first-name you unless you are first-naming back. Similarly, invite people to first name you—or use your surname—whenever the initial signals are unclear. It may take time and practice to feel comfortable saying things like, "Couldn't we keep this informal? I'd like you to call me Jenny," or, "in business situations I prefer to be addressed as Miss Peterson, Mr. Garfunkle."

When You Are Introduced as a Speaker

Find out what your introducer plans to say about you ahead of time; help her with your name and/or title and forestall offensive terminology, such as "the girl who . . ." State, if necessary, that you do not wish to be described by how many children you have, or other personal information, unless it is relevant for this group. Be prepared to offer suggestions—a good verbal résumé— to give her a "handle" on you. Mention what talent, skill or knowledge you have that qualifies you to make *this* speech.

The remarks your introducer makes about you set you up for the group. The introduction creates an impression that may last throughout your talk; do justice to yourself by making sure the impression is one that will help, not one you have to overcome—or correct—before you can launch into your talk.

Look alive during everything being said from the podium; you appear unattractively self-centered if the first time you glance up is when your hear your name mentioned. Keep your ears—and your expression—perked up for all the group's announcements and previous speakers.

Responding to an Introduction

Usually, "Thank you, Sally," or "Thank you" to the audience in appreciation for their applause of welcome is adequate. Often, you won't want to say "thank you" at all. Just smile at the introducer as a thanks and/or shake hands.

If you need to make a speech of response before beginning your prepared remarks, you will have to make it up on the spot. Take your cue from the introduction. If it was formal, answer formally, addressing the person who welcomed you by name, but keeping your head turned to the microphone and toward the audience for most of what you say. Be brief and sincere. "I appreciate your making me feel so welcome. I'm glad to be with you," is usually ample response. Giving the impression that you enjoy being there and enjoy the job of giving a speech is more important than the actual words you choose.

Introducing a Speaker

Prepare an introduction as you would prepare any formal speech. Find out about the audience, make arrangements with the liaison person (although often the introducer *is* the liaison), find quotations, edit the introduction (sometimes with the assistance of the speaker herself), and time your out-loud rehearsals.

What's It for?

Most introductions simply welcome your guest and tell the audience something about her. Before you sit down to compose your introduction, however, consider further possibilities. To clarify your hidden agenda (if you have one) ask yourself:

What kind of speaker/audience relationship do I want to establish?

What is the group's attitude toward the speaker? Her topic?

Do I want the group to identify with her? Do I want them to feel that she is one of us? That she is an honored guest?

Is my group so skeptical or hostile that I prefer to establish her as an authority, to enhance her credibility or to emphasize her credentials so that she will be received more respectfully?

Is it better to establish a serious or light tone for the meeting? Is the audience a willing or captive group?

Do I want my remarks to *deflect controversy* by answering objections before they are raised?

Do I want my remarks to *stimulate controversy*, to plant questions in the hearers' minds?

Do I need to prepare the audience with specific information so they can form expectations? Is there some factual groundwork I need to lay so that the speaker's message will be clearer?

Do I want to relax the audience, or do I prefer to make them sit up in alert anticipation?

How well known is the speaker to this group? What do they know about her already that I won't need to repeat in the introduction?

Obviously, the emphasis and emotional tone of your introduction must reflect the circumstances of the particular audience and the particular speaker. However, the *usual* purposes of an introduction are to: inform the audience about the speaker so that they will be prepared; persuade the audience to listen; create enthusiasm for what is to come; make the speaker feel welcome and encouraged; and relax her so she can do a good job.

Interviewing the Speaker

As a courtesy to the speaker and as a safeguard for yourself, contact the speaker in person, by telephone or in a letter well before the day of her presentation. An experienced speaker will often suggest excellent quotes, colorful facts or descriptive language you can use in her introduction (that is, she may have a good verbal résumé). Ask if she has publicity material or a bio. Do *not* trust anything you read about her in the newspapers. Check out all information coming from *any* source other than the speaker herself.

A few questions will elicit helpful facts from less experienced speakers. Try open-ended questions to uncover key phrases:

> "How would someone else describe you in one or two sentences?"
> "Is there something about you hardly anyone knows that you would like more people to know about?"
> "How do you see your role as a _____?"
> "Ideally, what do you want to happen/come out of this speaking engagement?"

It is ordinarily a good idea to run through the entire introduction you are planning with the speaker to doublecheck for accuracy or duplication. If you don't, you may ruin your speaker's opening. For instance, if you choose to explain in your introduction that Mary Healthcare, a well-known doctor, is a bicycle expert you might say, "You may be surprised that she will be speaking today on bike repair, not on why bike riding is healthful!" What if Mary's opening line is something like, "You may be surprised that I am going to talk about bike repair rather than the reasons bike riding is good for our health." Ouch.

It may be utterly impossible for you to respect the speaker's wishes to include in (or delete from) your introduction something she requests. Decline her suggestion and invite *her* to give the audience the information you decided to omit.

What Do You Say?

Usually: your name, her name, the occasion, her topic.
Sometimes: how long she will talk, whether she will answer questions when she has finished speaking.

Skip the Formulas

"Good afternoon, I'm Joanie Baloney, and welcome to the third annual county-wide Grimacing Contest. I would like to introduce our main speaker for today, Adele Twitch," etcetera. This clichéd format is boring. Try to get around saying such unoriginal lines as "Good morning, ladies and gentlemen"; "We have with us today"; "It is my great pleasure to introduce"; "I have the honor of introducing." Do not say "The woman who..."

Whenever we hear someone announce, "Tonight's speaker really needs no introduction," we want to say "Good! Sit down!"

Be Brief

If you must precede your introduction with "housekeeping" announcements, make it snappy. The audience came to hear the speaker, not the introducer, so don't remain on stage for a disproportionate length of time. On the other hand, don't repeat the old saw "Well, you came to hear her, not me, so I'm going to sit down now..." Avoid self-deprecation in any circumstances.

The introduction to a five to fifteen minute speech should

take from thirty seconds to one minute. For a main speaker, or someone who will be speaking for twenty minutes or longer, one and a half to two minutes should be ample to arouse audience attention and curiosity without stealing the speaker's thunder. We cannot think of any circumstances that would justify an introduction that lasts longer than three minutes.

Tell the Audience What the Speaker Will Talk About

Don't omit the title of her talk, or her subject if she hasn't given the speech a formal title, even if this information is already printed in a program for the audience to read.

Repeat the Speaker's Name Several Times

Be sure to say her name at the beginning of your introduction. Repeat it at the end as a cue to speaker and audience alike that your introduction is over.

Get the Name Right

Ask the speaker what name she prefers to be called. Do not assume that Doctor Katherine Smith wants you to use her title. Perhaps she prefers to be known to *this* group as "Kate."

Perhaps the speaker has recently resumed using her birth name, and the "Smith" you know her by is now completely wrong. Ask!

Practice pronouncing a difficult name with the speaker until you can say it correctly. It is not funny to mispronounce a person's name, and less amusing still to tease or joke about it.

Be especially careful about using first names. Robin Lakoff says,

I feel that, other things being equal, there is greater likelihood of hearing Gloria Steinem called "Gloria" by someone who does not know her very well than of hearing Norman Mailer called "Norman" under the same conditions... This usage is perhaps to be compared with the tradition of calling children freely by their first names....*

Include Anecdotes and Quotations

A chronological recitation of accomplishments and credentials is boring and flavorless. Give the speaker a personality by deleting a few degrees, jobs and honors, and filling in a story to illustrate what kind of person she is, what she actually does all day, or what impresses you most about her. Quote her, if possible, or quote someone else's remarks about her.

What Not to Say

Sometimes the speaker's personal relationships or physical appearance can be relevant information for an introduction. If you are introducing the woman whose daughter is the first girl to play Little League in your town, and your audience is the Women's Athletic Association, then perhaps your speaker's status as "mother of" may be appropriate information.

If the audience is Weight Watchers, your speaker's dress size may constitute a "bona fide occupational qualification" for this particular speech.

But, in general, do not describe a woman in terms of her personal relationships and do not typecast her in terms of her physical appearance. Be sure you tell about what *she* does, not what her husband does or what her supervisor does. Women often resent being defined as the "wife of" or "mother of" or "secretary to," and ordinarily prefer to have other credentials cited in an introduction.

* Robin Lakoff, *Language and Woman's Place*, p. 40.

It is not helpful to a speaker to be identified as a "trim blonde computer analyst" or by any kind of physical description. A physical evaluation is offensive, and it damages the speaker's credibility.

Do Not Belabor the Obvious

Use your time to tell the audience something special that they may not already know about the speaker. If the speaker is well known to—or a member of—your group, many of the facts you would customarily include when introducing a stranger should be omitted.

Except for the subject of the talk, delete data, including biographical information, that is printed in the program.

Do Not Praise the Speaker's Speaking Ability

If you get the group fixated on her style, they may miss her content. Why distract the audience from what she has to say? Besides, wouldn't it make *you* nervous to hear about what a terrific job you are going to do?

Be careful about praising a speaker's wit, fame and intelligence. If the audience expects wit they may wait for jokes and be disappointed. If the group hears how smart the speaker is, they may become defensive or belligerent ("She's no smarter than I am,"). Fame is not a characteristic of the speaker; fame reflects the mood or taste of the press more than it reflects the speaker's good traits or hard work.

Don't Overpraise

An introduction that states "I'm glad you are with us" is fine. A gushing introduction embarrasses everyone. Maybe you *do* feel "honored and privileged to be on the same platform with Arline Scott," but if you carry on about it, your case of the "gratefuls" may cause the audience to squirm, or perhaps even resent the speaker enough to resist her ideas. ("If she's so much better than we are, so bloody superior in every way, then what's she doing in the company of such simple peasants in the first place? Is this a charity call?")

Glowing words delivered in a matter-of-fact tone are not so effective as a few simple words spoken sincerely. The spirit of good feeling counts the most.

Introducing Men

Women who would never act submissive or flirtatious at work sometimes catch themselves regressing to subordinate behavior when introducing men at civic affairs or club meetings that are relatively social in character.

> "We're so *lucky* to have Steve Manymachos with us today (smirk). He is unbelievably kind to take time out of his busy schedule of important meetings to come and talk to us (simper)."

As an extra precaution, read through the introduction you are planning and substitute the name of a woman. Does the introduction now sound fawning?

If you know the man well, call him "Norman"; do not entitle a man in an informal situation if you wouldn't automatically entitle a woman.

Keep Yourself Out of It

Your pet opinions on the speaker's topic may not be what the audience needs to know. Your relationship to the speaker is probably not relevant, either. Who cares if you've known her for twenty years, and why are you bringing it up? To bask in her reflected glory?

The exception to your low profile as introducer might be

when the group knows and trusts you, but is suspicious of the speaker or her topic. In these circumstances it is nice to say "my friend . . ."

Rehearse Your Rituals

Whether the speaker is new and nervous, or an old hand at public appearances, tell her in advance exactly what is going to happen and what the sequence of events will be. Remind her what the last line of your introduction says so she will be ready to come forward. If you are planning to shake hands, say so. *She* may be planning to have both hands full of notes and visual aids. Besides, if she isn't expecting a handshake, she may not see your extended arm and both of you will look awkward.

Don't Look at the Speaker

Turn toward the person you are welcoming just once. Remember that you are addressing the audience, not the speaker. Just as new speakers sometimes stare at their visual aids and forget the audience, new introducers sometimes gaze at the speaker while addressing remarks to the group.

Cue the Audience

In any formal presentation you want to let the audience know when it's time to clap. You do this by selecting words that are final-sounding, inflecting your voice in the wrap-up, and using body language that signifies a change.

In an introduction you also cue the audience by repeating the speaker's name at the end, and initiating the applause for her.

In casual settings, take a step back from the lectern when you've completed your remarks, and clap for a second while you watch the speaker approach you. Leave to take your seat after this pause.

In formal situations (a banquet, a large audience, a stage setting), you applaud until the speaker reaches your side, shake her hand in welcome and quickly return to your place. Although it may seem strange to shake hands with a speaker you've spent two hours chatting with over dinner, and who is also your best friend, do so if the occasion is formal.

Sample Introductions

Sometimes an introducer is asked to perform miracles. What if your speaker tells you only that her name is Stephanie DeVivo and that she is a purchasing agent with an insurance firm; what can you do with that?

Ask a few questions to see if you can come up with something funny or unusual to put color in this woman's poor verbal résumé.

Let's imagine the audience is a group of working mothers who are considering the formation of a neighborhood child care center.

Speaker's full name	"Apparently Stephanie DeVivo is just	
Relationship with audience; trust her, she is one of us	like the rest of us; she lives approximately thirty-two hours per day. She has two jobs, one as a Purchasing Assistant for the Slippery Banana Insurance Company in Winchester, and the	*Her I.D.; a credential*
	other as the mother of a ten-year-old daughter. Please join me in extending a	*Her credential to this group*
		Applause cue

Light mood, tone	warm welcome to an excellent representative of the vitamin and black coffee club. Stephanie?" *Name repeated*

This introduction is very informal. It has the quality of an introduction of a personal friend to other personal friends.

Now let's compare two introductions of the same woman to the same group to see how the introducer's motives alter the wording.

The group is gathered for the regular monthly meeting of federal employees. About thirty people assemble with their sandwiches in brown bags to hear speakers on personnel issues of interest to government workers. There is ample advertising in advance, including how long the speakers will talk and whether she/he will take questions from the audience.

The speaker has told you her name and her topic, "The Upward Mobility Program and How It Works."

Full name	"Barbara Harris sees herself as a community worker in Roxbury, dealing particularly with teenage children. Her current job as an F.D.A. file clerk won't get her there, but her studies in sociology and psychology under the Upward Mobility Program will.	*Her credentials to this group. In this homogeneous gathering, everyone will know that F.D.A. stands for Food and Drug Administration*
Cue to clap	Let's greet an ambitious and far sighted colleague. Barbara?"	*Informal gathering, first-name basis*

The purpose of this introduction is to qualify the speaker in a way that will encourage the audience to identify with her. She is established not as a Supergrade coming down from on high to pontificate about what a program is supposed to do, but as a worker who knows the reality behind the rhetoric because she is *in* the program.

"This afternoon we are going to hear the truth about the Upward Mobility Program. We have all read the directives regarding what the program is supposed to do, but today for the first time we have a speaker who is qualified to tell us from personal experience what Upward Mobility is actually achieving. Barbara Harris is a file clerk with the Food and Drug Administration and her ambition is to become a community worker in Roxbury. Before the Question and Answer session, she will talk to us for about fifteen minutes about how Upward Mobility may—or may not—help an employee change career ladders. Everyone join me, please, in welcoming Ms. Harris."

Left margin notes:

Credential

What to expect

Why we should listen

Clapping cue

Right margin notes:

Startling, loaded words for a tame, stuffy group. Attention-getting

Special occasion

Her full name

Name repeated. Note title; respect and authority desired. Cues audience to address her formally in Q & A

Here the introducer establishes the ground rules for this group in terms of time and format. Otherwise, the information in this introduction is the same. It is the mood that has changed drastically. This introduction acknowledges the audience's informed skepticism surrounding Barbara Harris' topic while establishing the image of Ms. Harris herself as a somewhat tough-minded insider who is to be taken seriously. The language is more formal, and the introducer has taken pains to create a sense of occasion for the audience and to make the experience of listening to Ms. Harris seem special. The mood is less warm than in the first example, and while Ms. Harris could praise or blame the Upward Mobility Program, some curiosity may be aroused about which she will do. In the first Barbara Harris example, our excitement about hearing her stems from the enthusiasm we all feel for a success story, and one that could be our own someday. In the second example, the introducer has appealed to our consumer instincts instead: is the program a gyp or does it work?

Introducing Panel Members

Moderating a panel can be a real challenge to your ingenuity. Your goal is to dream up four or five introductions that have life, provide meaningful information, treat each panelist equally while accommodating their different personalities, and to solve the problems in establishing several speaker/audience relationships.

An Introduction Is a Speech

The spotlight may only be on you for a moment, but introductions are excellent practice for larger speaking parts.

CHAPTER NINE

Speaking Impromptu

An impromptu speech is any utterance, no matter how short, which is totally unprepared and spoken without notes. Our definition includes not only what you say in job interviews but also what you say to the butcher, what you say when your horse wins the race, and what you say when you find out your lover is cheating. But, you say, that means I'm making impromptu speeches all the time, every minute of my life. That is exactly right. Of course it matters more in some circumstances than in others that you sound intelligent and stay poised; a job interview is quite different from a talk with a casual acquaintance. Nevertheless, those who care about how they talk all the time do better when it really counts. It pays to remember that any time you talk "off the top of your head" you are making a speech. The ability to speak clearly and effectively without preparation is probably admired more than any other speaking skill. In our classes, it is always this skill students refer to when they say, "She is so articulate." We all fear that in important circumstances we won't be articulate, but will blank out or stumble around. Actually, once you know the technique and practice it, it is easy.

The trick of impromptu speaking is not being able to think fast, it's being able to decide, to commit yourself fast. You must decide which of the many things that pop into your mind you actually want to say and the best way to say it. Whatever you decide, commit yourself firmly and irrevocably. This isn't easy for women to do. Unfortunately, some of us have been so squelched, ridiculed and scoffed at that we actually believe we can't think of a thing to say. For example, if the speech you would like to make in response to an interviewer's questions about your child-care arrangements is "What's it to you, you stupid jerk?" then it isn't surprising that you think you don't have anything to say. In fact, a different version of that response is a perfect answer, but if you block the original thought you'll never work up the appropriate way to say it. Whether it is because we're afraid of sounding foolish, or because we know for sure our listeners aren't going to like what we have to say, it is doubt and worry that ties our tongue. Often we end up trying to not say what we want to say and our sidetracking, backtracking and "tact" make us sound very confused. Commit yourself to saying what you think. Impromptu speaking isn't difficult because you are dim, it's difficult because you don't have confidence in your opinions.

And while we are attacking common misconceptions about being "articulate," let us also say that impromptu speaking isn't difficult because you are under- or miseducated. All too often in our classes women report that their fear of impromptu speaking is based on an underlying uneasiness about their education. Many of us have an exaggerated respect for education and what it can do, perhaps because for years women were denied access to it. In any case, there is no direct connection between years of education and eloquence. While we would be the last to deny that the best way to become glib is an Ivy League education, the ease and confidence come from the experience of power and respect (the experience of being treated as one of the elite, a future leader of the world) and not from the books. You can be eloquent with simple everyday words. It is feeling and conviction that make a speech moving. For example:

"No, I won't do it. I don't want to."

"I won't listen to what you say about her, she is my friend."

"Please, help me, I'm afraid."

"I am very angry."

If you want to improve your vocabulary the place to begin is among your friends. Most of us abuse our relationships by talking "lazy" when we feel comfortable. "Wow, I really had a nice day. I had the nicest lunch with Joan, you know, at that nice place on Fifty-first. It's just so nice there, really fabulous." It doesn't take an expensive education to treat your friends better. While big occasions often call for the simplest language, everyday life could be greatly enlivened by an animated vocabulary.

When you are unprepared, it is absolutely vital that you maintain poise, which means relaxed posture, audible voice, good pitch, direct eye contact and NO APOLOGIES. (Does this sound familiar?) Any audience will forgive more if the speaker maintains her poise. If your poise and self-control are superb you can just stand there and say "I don't know," and give people the impression that you're brilliant, and furthermore, it wasn't worth knowing.

Appearing confident can, however, take you only so far if you intend to try to say something. It is also important to have an organized mind. Organization depends on the proper structure. Just as you need certain apparatus to organize an office (file cabinets, Rolodex files, shelves), you need a framework on which to hang your random darting thoughts. There are several ways to do this. We suggest the following.

Think first of your conclusion. Knowing how the speech is going to end up is a comfort to those of us who are very scared and good discipline for those of us who would just as soon never end up at all but go on talking forever. In addition, if everything you say leads toward a conclusion, that alone is organization. A conclusion, a point, a focus, a punch line is vital.

This approach is not "natural." Most of us try to organize our talk through a chronological order or, worse, simply pile on evidence as it occurs to us. The order in which things happened in time provides simple organization for certain kinds of stories, folk songs and jokes. (Also certain informative talks. See Chapter Five.) It is boring, though, and lacks focus. The order in which events occurred may not be the most interesting aspect of the events. "And then I... and then I... and then I..." describes what you did but not who you are, what you want or what you mean. People arrested at the chronological level respond with the "then, then, then" approach to any topic, no matter how little it lends itself to this treatment. For example:

Question: "Tell us a little about yourself."

Answer: "Well, I was born in Arkansas, but then I went to New York. I got a job as a file clerk for Time, Inc., and then I was promoted to secretary with some research, and then to researcher and then...

Question: "Do you like carrots?"

Answer: "Well, I used to like carrots but then I had too many at once and now I don't like them much."

Question: "Would you introduce the speaker?"

Answer: "Eleanor Bowen is the speaker tonight. She used to be on the PTA but then she got elected to the School Committee and she is going to tell us about closing the schools."

Your listeners shouldn't have to struggle to understand why you are saying what you are saying. If people often say, "What's the point?" or "Get to the point," you probably need practice focusing. (Saying, "Get to the point!" is also a put-down. If you know you *are* getting to the point and this person interrupts you often, just tell him to shut up.)

How can the examples above be focused more effectively?

Begin by asking yourself, "What is the most important thing about what I am going to say?" In the first example, the most important point is whatever it is about you that you would most like the questioner to know. Let's say this is a job interview with a publishing house. You want them to know about your interest in and experience with books. You might focus something like this:

> "All my life I have loved books as a reader. Now, after five years' experience in publishing, I love the process of putting books and magazines together. I think of myself as a book mechanic."

In the second example, you want to answer the question with "yes" or "no" and support your conclusion with the main reason:

> "I overdosed on carrots once. Besides, they are sweet and thick. I hate them."

In the third case, it is important for the audience to know why the speaker has come:

> "Many of us have been troubled by the city's decision to close several elementary schools because of declining enrollment. We are pleased, therefore, to have Eleanor Bowen from the School Committee as our speaker tonight. She will be able to answer many of our questions."

An alert reader will have noticed that the conclusion, while thought of first, is spoken last. This order does make sense but is almost never followed. Most of us eagerly announce our conclusion first and then go on to try to support it. Unfortunately, this means that those who disagree with the conclusion don't stop to listen to the evidence but interrupt or just tune out. If you put your reasons for thinking what you think first, you have a better chance.

A conclusion organization stating one or two pieces of supporting evidence and then the conclusion helps us avoid talking ourselves into a corner. We have all been in circumstances or moods when we felt so inadequate and humble that we go on and on apologizing and explaining until we are exhausted.

> "Gee, I never really thought about it. I don't uh, well, I guess I believe that, uh, suicide, I mean, this is dumb but I guess I really think it's wrong, you know? Well, maybe not wrong, exactly, but not fair. You see, I..."

That speech, accompanied by a lot of shrugging, grimacing and a little laugh on the end doesn't convey strength and conviction. Don't be afraid to stop, even if you feel that what you've already said is awful. You probably can't redeem it by going on and on. It doesn't matter who is making you feel inadequate or why; if you are in the habit of making your point and shutting up, your lack of confidence won't show as much. This is easier when you have your conclusion firmly in mind.

In impromptu situations you can begin with a dull remark, a generalization or practically anything that allows you to stall for time. Your priorities are to think of a conclusion and some supporting evidence. Before you open your mouth, you think your conclusion. Let's say you quickly decide that your conclusion is "I think suicide is wrong." Begin with a generalization while you compose your reasons.

> "There are so many young people taking their own lives. (Generalization.) But suicide extinguishes hope (reason) often in cases where time and maturity would have changed everything (reason). I believe it is wrong."

People will jump in with all kinds of arguments about who should be able to commit suicide and special circumstances and what do you mean "wrong" and so forth, but you *have* gotten them to listen to your reasons. If you simply say "I think it's wrong for kids to kill themselves," someone will surely shout "How can you say that?" and you will end up feeling defensive. Save the conclusions for last so you can build your case on your own terms.

Although it may feel artificial and stilted, it is helpful to begin your impromptu speeches with "Because..." until you have retrained yourself. For example:

Question: "Do you favor the Supreme Court decision on abortion?"

Answer: "Because birth control is still difficult to get, difficult to use and inefficient, and because unwanted children are a personal tragedy and often a financial burden on the taxpayer, I certainly do favor the Court's decision."

With practice, the "Because . . . because . . . because . . ." will become silent. Soon you will routinely arrange your ideas in a well-organized fashion. First, a general remark to buy time. Then, because, because, because. Finally, your conclusion.

A longer impromptu speech works on the same principle as a short one. You have a major point to make. Each supporting point can be longer and have supporting points of its own. You may add three or four subtopics and stay fairly well organized. It is impossible, however, for most people to speak effectively for more than five minutes or so without some kind of notes. In situations like meetings, long telephone calls, or interviews where you may wish or be asked to speak at length, have a notebook with you so you can make quick notes while you listen to others talk.

Better yet, make your speeches as un-impromptu as possible. Think through ahead of time what is likely to happen and make notes. For example, if you attend a meeting to discuss the preservation of a local historical building, ask yourself: Who is going to be there? What will their positions be? What are the arguments pro and con likely to sound like? Then prepare yourself by writing down the points you think are important and practice saying a few words about each. If you get into the habit of preparing yourself, you can virtually eliminate the whole idea of impromptu. (The term for speaking without notes but with plenty of preparation is "extemporaneous.")

Make yourself a list of random topics and practice short impromptus until you are good at it. Do it out loud. It is too easy to sound terrific in your own head. (When something brilliant that you should have said comes to you AFTER it is too late to say it, practice saying it anyway, out loud. Tell it to a friend. Write it down.) Your list might be based on general topics that come up in conversation all the time such as:

money
crime
sex
psychology
motherhood
sickness and death

or you might make it more specific and difficult. For example:

the defense budget
the energy crisis
the job market
prices of goods
transportation

Your first reaction to a topic with which you are utterly unfamiliar is probably to keep quiet. That's a good idea sometimes, but other times you are forced to speak. For those special occasions you must learn the fine art of subtly changing the subject. Try some gliding over phrases like:

"That's a good point and we could also think about..."

"I'm glad you asked because it gives me a chance to talk about..."

"That reminds me..."

Simply launch into your own topic and ignore the subject offered you. Many politicians abuse this technique and dodge more questions than they answer. We do not suggest that you bullshit people (much). There are circumstances, however, when it is better not to be obedient to a demand for information. (See Chapter Eleven.)

When you practice, it is a good idea to concentrate on topics that always give you trouble:

What to say to the man who is putting his swinish hands on you

What to say to a friend who hates and attacks another friend

How to say a few words about yourself (see Chapter Eight)

How to get the landlord, who never fixes anything, to fix . . .

What to say to the arresting officer

Or to the thirteen-year-old babysitter who always wants to let you know later whether she will sit on Saturday night

Or when your lover's mother calls

Or when your husband has started to call you "Oh, Harriet, for crissake . . ."

Or when your five-year-old asks, "Mommy, will I ever die . . ."

Let's take the landlord example. You start with your conclusion. Probably in these circumstances your point is some sort of mild threat, say that you are going to talk to a lawyer. Give one or two reasons and your conclusion.

> "Mr. Smith, when I got up this morning there was ice in the toilet. My daughter has had a cold all winter. It is against the law not to provide heat, and if I am not warm in one hour I am going to call my lawyer."

(You don't have to have a lawyer to say this, you can always get one if the landlord refuses to turn up the heat.)

An enormous vocabulary isn't necessary. You don't have to be original and clever. If your message is short, to the point and spoken without apology, stumbling or embarrassment, you have won a great victory.

The wonderful thing about impromptu speaking, as opposed to formal speaking, is that we have lots of opportunities to practice and can become really expert. You don't have to go looking for opportunities to practice and improve; they will come looking for you. For the perfect opportunity, see the next chapter.

CHAPTER TEN

Talking in Groups

"Is this meeting necessary, or would a party do just as well?" is the first question to ask yourself if you are in charge of a group. Meetings are called ostensibly to inform people or to decide something. Actually, these purposes are often only the pretext for getting together. The real reason may be to rub shoulders, to give the appearance of action, or to give the boss a chance to lord it over everyone.

In addition, most meetings are boring, inefficient and last longer than they need to. If everyone knows all the work will be done by a small committee anyhow, the meeting shouldn't be called.

The woman who arranges and chairs a meeting ignores the human needs of the participants at her peril. You must allow some room for stroking and fun. If you don't, the proceedings will be disrupted by whispering, joking, socializing, arguing, people bringing up the same point over and over, interrupting, or asking for unnecessary discussion when the time comes to vote.

In short, unless there is a compelling reason to call your people together, don't do it. If you do call a meeting, remember your objective is to be effective on two fronts: to get a task accomplished and to satisfy the affiliation needs of the participants.

How to Run a Meeting

When power is not spelled out according to rules that all can see, it is hidden and may be based on very strange dynamics indeed. For example, who is the loudest. Or who never says anything but is sleeping with the loudest. For task-oriented groups we recommend explicit rules of decision-making that are formalized. Old-fashioned parliamentary procedure (*Robert's Rules of Order*) is one way to attempt a fair hearing for all, but it is no guarantee. Parliamentary procedure can also be manipulated to block the wishes of the great majority, to embarrass someone who makes a technical error or to prevent someone from getting a hearing. The purposes of parliamentary procedure (to protect the right of the minority to voice opinions and to prevent hasty action) are sometimes distorted.

Since most formal gatherings (such as the House of Representatives, School Boards, plenary sessions at large conferences) use *Robert's Rules of Order*, we suggest that you familiarize yourself with them. They are available in paperback, or you may prefer to get the College Outline Series explanation. Professional parliamentarians sometimes conduct classes in the procedure. Those who don't understand the rules seldom get their motions voted on and passed.

Since almost any system of preparation and order is better than none, we suggest that at the very least you establish rules for introducing topics and for taking turns in speaking.

At many meetings the majority of the attendees don't even know what the meeting is supposed to be about. This is inexcusable. Half-informed members can only reach half-baked decisions. A group needs to know ahead of time—two weeks in advance, if possible—what matters will be under discussion or up for a vote. This information, commonly called an agenda, should be written and distributed so that everyone will have a fair chance to think it over and to add ideas. Once a group votes to approve the agenda, the chair is justified in saying, "That will have to wait until another time. We are here to discuss . . ." "That" is anything suggested for discussion that is not on the agenda. Whoever has appointed herself efficiency expert of the day can also ask from time to time, "Could we try to stick to the agenda?" If there is no agenda, this person, as well as many other quieter people, will be angry and frustrated.

After you decide that you are going to meet and what you are going to accomplish when you meet, the next question is where you will meet. Setting is not a trivial matter. The emotional tone of the get-together may be determined at the moment you decide whether to scatter people in a huge hall or pack them into a conference room. People, like molecules, heat up when compressed. If you want the issue to be cooled down, spread out. If you think there is apathy and you want to generate excitement, crowd.

There is also a psychology to comfort. Roomy, soft chairs, large ashtrays, lunch on the sideboard, carpeting and water pitchers encourage smugness. Hold meetings in fancy settings when you have to tell people very bad news. Discomfort (up to a point) sharpens the wit.

Microphones are important for a large group in an auditorium. If you want to make sure people can hear one another, you will need a microphone handy in each aisle.

If you notice chattering and a tendency to shift from topic to topic, ask yourself if the setting is too informal. Don't hold meetings in-house unless the subject of your meeting is directly relevant to the day-to-day conduct of your organization. Training sessions, quarterly meetings and so forth should be held far enough away from your ordinary place of business so that those who fancy themselves vital to some other proceedings can't run in and out, go back to the office, make calls, check on things. Distance from the job site is particularly important when those attending the meeting are not very powerful and are likely to be called away at their boss's whim.

It should go without saying that it is in poor taste to hold a meeting in a club that discriminates against women or in a conference room several floors from the ladies' room or in any other location that will make women uncomfortable.

It is now customary to divide up a room into clean air sections and dirty air sections. Nonsmokers tend to leave early if the smokers aren't segregated.

Once assembled, the meeting needs a record keeper. (Of course, an alert attendee will keep her own record as well.) In small informal groups, this person usually volunteers to make notes on the main pros and cons of discussion, and on all formal motions, resolutions or decisions. In larger groups the record keeper or secretary takes official minutes. Sometimes it helps people to think more clearly if agenda, meeting progress and main ideas are visible. Newsprint paper tacked up around the walls, flip charts, a good blackboard, anything that everyone can see is an improvement over somebody's private steno pad. Public record keeping discourages rambling, repetitiveness, and quarrels by making group activity clear.

Opening the Proceedings

When you are in charge of a meeting it is up to you to state the purpose of the meeting and set the stage for fruitful discussion. That means you must take charge forcefully. It will not do for the chair to shilly-shally about as though she wasn't sure exactly what she ought to be doing. (Practice your opening remarks. This is a speech.)

Introduce yourself, make a few orienting remarks to get the group ready to start thinking about the problems at hand, and open the floor.

Probably the least welcome words in English are "Well, why don't we all introduce ourselves." If the group members don't know one another at all, introductions might be useful. The inarticulate hemming and hawing of twenty or more self-introducers, however, is of interest only to a speech teacher. (Naturally, when *you* attend a meeting, you come on like a pro because you have read the chapters on introductions and impromptus and practiced your verbal résumé.) As the chair, you probably know everyone by name. Call on people by name and/or ask each person to announce who she is whenever she speaks. Round robin introductions are hick. Name tags, however, are splendid, especially if the names on them are in large black letters and are legible from across the room.

Running the Show

Somebody once said, "A well-defined question answers itself." There is great truth in this. Before the group makes any decision and especially before you put anything to a vote, be sure everyone understands why there is a problem. In most meetings everyone votes and goes home mad before the question or the issue is ever properly defined. It is your job as chair to facilitate the definition of the question. "Do we agree the problem can be defined as ... ?"

A meeting called to grapple with an issue that is eventually defined as a nonissue is still a fruitful meeting. "Josephine has stated that the condition of the front lawn bores her and is not a proper matter of discussion for this group. Do any of you care to take a different stand?"

Ask questions, summarize often and keep the ball rolling. You maintain efficient deliberations by crystallizing contributions, agreements and points of conflict.

"So far, I have heard suggestions that we cover the lawn with horse manure, that we reseed it, and that we pave it over. Does one method seem more practical?"

"We've heard permanence, parking space and swift results in support of the proposal to pave over the front lawn. Is there further comment?"

You can also ask the recorder to summarize part of the discussion for the group.

A good chair is impartial; encourage participation by remaining neutral at the helm. If you cannot stick to the role of unbiased leader, let someone else take over the chair while you enter the debate. Your job is to facilitate a convivial interchange of ideas and differences, not to be a central speaker yourself. Piloting a meeting means motivating others to contribute, and it sometimes takes plenty of self-control to play the waiting game. Try, "Do any of you care to express the view I've heard that horse manure is expensive?" to get the group talking. If you wait long enough someone will speak up.

If a participant offers an unsupported opinion, you can ask, "Can you give us your reasons for that statement?" Or you can cue the others that an argument bears evaluation by saying, "Joseph has offered a broad generalization. Is there any discussion?" This may prompt someone to request Joseph's evidence or reasoning.

Remember a rushed conclusion only forces you to rethink the issue. "Apparently we approve of the suggestion to cover the lawn with horse manure. Before we vote, I believe we should test the decision by discussing the consequences or weaknesses of the idea. Are there any negatives or weaknesses we haven't thought of?"

Even if the conclusion of the meeting is obvious, it is still the chair's job to state the exact results anyway: the areas of agreement, the areas of disagreement, the action plans. People like to go away with a formal "finished" feeling.

Troublemakers

People go to meetings for a variety of reasons, not all of them helpful to the task at hand. Meetings are attended by professional negatives who are antieverything and by grandstanders who want to provide a running commentary on each point. Neglected, confused, sullen or withdrawn members may become disruptive. Look around, watch people's faces and see if you can head off trouble before it starts.

If someone is shaking her head violently, say, "You don't seem to agree, Jackie. What do you think?" Draw out those who are reluctant to speak up unless invited. They often have something valuable to contribute.

You must also quiet a domineering pushy member of the group who talks all of the time—especially if he isn't listening to what anyone else is saying. It takes nerve, but here is what to say:

> "Harry, I'm going to acknowledge the other raised hands before you or other previous speakers talk for a second time."
>
> "Will the speaker please conclude his remarks."
>
> "Jim, will you explain how your remark relates to the agenda item? We are considering item four. Are you addressing that point?"

There are also people in every group who will enthusiastically and pleasantly address every single question *at length* unless curbed. It is sometimes easier to summon the nerve to silence a participant who is clearly the overbearing type than to silence a nice person who is simply overeager.

It may help to have a private word with the person who takes up too much floor time: "I hope you will understand my dilemma. If I am not successful in eliciting the participation of everyone, I will not have done my job. Please hold off on your contributions for the rest of the day, and let me see if I can't get the others to speak up. I appreciate your enthusiasm but I don't want to get a reputation as an unfair chairperson." Here is another approach: "If I am not successful in eliciting the participation of everyone, I am afraid you will wind up doing all the talking and thinking and possibly all the work as well. Please hold off on your contributions for the rest of the day. I want to see if I can get the others to speak up. I appreciate your ideas, but I don't want the group to become too dependent on you."

Then there are the Smilers. It doesn't take much experience

to learn that the woman who listens with a tight little smile on her face and who never objects to what is being said may be the woman who tries to undermine a meeting or a presentation indirectly, manipulatively—and definitely after the moderator or speaker is out of sight. After the meeting her favorite lines to her friends are, "I should have said..." or "Why didn't somebody object?" A smiler in a one-shot audience is best ignored. But if you meet the smiler again and again (as in a class you teach or a group you chair), then it is necessary to encourage her to state her objections openly. You can then negotiate, or persuade, or perhaps be convinced that she is in the right. If you discover that she will not embolden herself sufficiently to speak up, even with encouragement, you must neutralize her negativity in another way. Get her to state publicly, "No, I have no objections" or "Yes, I agree" or "No, I have nothing to say." A person who confines her disagreements to after-the-meeting criticism quickly discredits herself because it becomes obvious to the group that she is two-faced or does not have the courage of her convictions. Her peers will eventually react to her displeasure with, "Well, why didn't you speak up?" or "But you were asked what you thought."

Serious disrupters must be handled with authority. If worse comes to worst, ask the disrupters to leave.

Creative Listening

Clearly, nothing of value is going to be accomplished unless people listen to one another. Terrible disruptive quarrels break out because the combatants didn't hear or misheard one another. When we hear the entire implications of someone's idea, we don't scream "You're crazy!" because we usually find *parts* of the idea valuable—or at least concur with some of the values and reasons behind the idea.

Acid exchanges can result from permissive procedures. When the chair refuses to allow participants to speak out of turn or at cross-purposes, there may still be disagreements but there won't be war. In extreme cases it is necessary for the chair to remind everyone that it is okay to attack issues but not people; state that you will not tolerate coworkers (group members, the sisters, whoever) getting personal, calling names, or using disrespectful tones of voice.

When you moderate a volatile group or when the issues are likely to arouse strong feelings, insist that nobody quarrel with another person's opinion until the objector has paraphrased the opinion to the satisfaction of the speaker. As a participant, do not answer an objection yourself until you are sure that you are speaking to the *real* objection that is being raised. For example:

> "I think if we allow that sort of thinking to influence our decision then we have taken a serious step."

> "George, I think you are objecting to a certain point of view but I'm not sure what sort of thinking you mean."

> "I mean the so-called liberal point of view, which tries to solve problems by throwing money at them."

> "You mean we may be planning to spend more money than we have?"

> "Yes."

> "Well, I believe Mary is prepared to show all of you some of the budget figures for 1979–1980 that have been projected..."

Most of us go haywire when we hear insults, tags, labels and other nasty ways people have of objecting to what we have to say instead of listening to and answering the objection itself. It doesn't really injure your position after all to have your opponent call it "fascism" unless you then enter in with "knee jerk liberal," "bleeding heart," and so forth.

Making Your Presence Felt When You Are Not in Charge

Speak up early in every meeting. The longer you wait to talk the more you may feel that what you say has to be brilliant or profound. You can't concentrate on what the others are saying while you sit there trying to get up the nerve to speak. Once you have spoken it is easier to speak again. If there are five people in your group, try to do one-fifth of the talking.

If you often feel "But I have nothing to add" or "I can't think of anything to say" take a second look. If the truth is that you are scared to speak, then take our advice and say something, *anything* early in every meeting until speaking begins to get easier for you.

A good part of being effective is achieved by becoming visible. Are you trying to take up as little space as possible?

Spread out, relax your posture and make sure you aren't allowing others to encroach on your table space in meetings: spread your papers and other items out, too.

Notice where the power sits and integrate the space. Don't let all the "decision makers" clump together. Bosses love to hide behind large pieces of furniture (desks, conference tables). Nothing can make you feel like an accused murderer pleading with a judge faster than trying to talk across a wide expanse of mahogany. Move your chair right up next to theirs.

The action is in the direct line of vision of the person whom you most wish to impress, persuade or influence. At lectures or speeches or other occasions where the speaker or chairperson is in the front of the room, sit close to the front yourself. Your remarks will be solicited more often and the speaker will assume you are interested. Force yourself to overcome the old school habit of lurking in the back.

Unless record keeping is highly inappropriate—in revolutionary cells, groups of bank robbers, secret business deals, international spy rings—make notes. This is one way to look alert. Years of speaking, running workshops and meetings have proved to the authors that she who listens hardest gets the best the speaker has to offer. Speakers remember the note taker. They remember her name and what she said and they seek her out.

The opposite tactics, however, may be best at meetings

This poor woman's body is so wrapped up, she *can't* speak.

where everyone knows everyone else. For instance, is your note-taking excessive? Is it a way to shrink back, look busy and excuse yourself from speaking/participating?

If you are trying to stop feeling and looking subordinate and submissive, then you might stop paying such strict attention when the bigshots are speaking. You indicate your own lack of power by hanging on the boss's every word, leaning forward to hear. Similarly, remind yourself that those who dominate seldom really look at subordinates; don't become flustered when you receive minimal eye contact when you talk.

If the setting is informal (armchairs scattered around the room, for instance), or if you are at a meeting at a large table, sit where you will be seen and heard if you choose to speak. You may feel safest shlumping down beside your oldest and dearest friend, but the action is probably elsewhere.

Make yourself uncomfortable and sit down next to the powerful and influential instead. Notice that bosses feel comfortable sitting at the head of the table or the front of the room. (If you are the boss, you may feel uneasy up there because it is not a traditional "woman's place.")

If you get the creepy feeling that *nobody* is in charge, assert yourself. Do not sit politely by while the chairperson allows people to go off on tangents. Share leadership responsibility; take over for a while if the topic is jumping around, if the moderator fails to insist that speakers take turns, if the proceedings are being stifled by dominators. Is the room too cold? Are the dynamics impaired because people can't hear, or are seated too far from one another? Say, "Is anyone else cold? I'm going to turn up the heat. I see empty seats up front. Why don't we all move closer so we can hear better?" Do you notice that members of the group are consistently missing excellent points because they don't like the person who is making them (because her style is abrasive or she expresses herself shyly or she offends the group's dress norms or because she has been stereotyped by reputation)? Speak up!

Is there more action at the door than at the podium? Say, "I see latecomers bottled up at the door. I think it will be less disturbing if we stop for a minute till they come in and get settled."

And, finally, resist the pressure to conform. You don't want to leave a meeting thinking, "Why didn't I fight for it—it was the right idea."

The Sexual Politics of Floor Time

You are definitely not crazy if you hate to attend mixed-sex meetings. Men's dominance games are exceedingly unpleasant, and our strategies for instituting productive, egalitarian counteraction are only beginning to emerge.

The resistance to women is especially visible in previously all-male settings. Our presence breaks up the familiar all-boy routine, and even the most courteous of men can seldom stifle the urge to put the blame for everyone's social discomfort on us.

The first step toward undermining the present state of sexual politics is to examine what men do and what women do. The opinions we offer in this section are just that—opinions and impressions derived from personal experience. We hope our observations will make you feel less isolated in your struggle to effect the power relations around you. It is very easy to doubt your own feelings in situations like this.

Men's behavior is usually characterized by nonlistening and by conscious and unconscious attempts to extinguish women's verbal activity. Aside from the obvious example of the man who calls a meeting to "discuss" when he really wants to intimidate and direct, there are more subtle dynamics. Have you ever noticed the way men ignore a woman's idea but if a man later offers the same suggestion they acknowledge it as brilliant and credit it to him?

The failure to elaborate, to question, to discuss someone's idea—to simply ignore it—is a cruel form of put-down. In meetings of men and women topics or suggestions we initiate are dropped with a grunt; our base points are gotten away from without validation. It is very hard to keep throwing out opinions that are not returned. Men don't respond. They wait until a woman finishes talking then they say what they had planned to say all along without reference to what she has just offered.

Men argue a lot. Their jousting matches with abstractions, their proving of points and scoring of points, cause lots of noise but little real connecting. If everything you say is ignored or argued to death, you may soon become silent unless you can find support for your ideas from other women.

Unfortunately, women—like any newcomers to power—feel the pressure to be correct, while men feel much freer. Notice how men support each other's unfocused statements or hasty judgments while a woman sits silently, caring that what she says be "right."

Women seem more capable of real exchange, that is, we

try to get on another person's wavelength, think *along with* someone else who is speaking. As a result, we are sometimes changed, as men so seldom are, during or after a conversation. Women encourage a speaker who is trying to tell something by nodding and saying uh-huh, by not interrupting, by "hooking up." We listen so well that we can frequently complete the speaker's sentence for her if she gets stuck. Our responses often include self-disclosure to build on what the speaker said and develop her themes. We show our support by asking questions, encouraging the other, volleying rather than dropping an idea. Where men dispute or ignore, women acknowledge and apply. "I'd like to tie in with what Sharon said earlier."

We believe it is important to avoid copying men. It would be a shame to see women indulge in aggressive joking and tyrannical "Are *you* trying to tell *me?*" male language. Instead we hope that recognition will grow for womanly styles of sharing information, reducing tension in groups, and working together.

We also believe that an essential ingredient of healthful change is women supporting women. Here is what we think we women can do for ourselves and one another in meetings.

Don't let a woman feel she's put her point into outer space. Pick up on it, acknowledge it, recognize that she has spoken. We may either disagree or build on what is said, but if we don't respond to each other most of what we say will fall into the abyss. Men simply don't see us; we can make one another feel respected, noticed and appreciated.

Protest when a man interrupts you. Interrupt a man who is interrupting a woman. "Senator, I don't believe Ms. Thill has quite finished." "Larry, Marcia is talking; we want to hear what she is saying." When a man starts to interrupt, all of the women present should keep their eyes fastened on the woman who was talking—if you turn to look at the interrupter, you acknowledge that he has the floor, and you give your consent to his interruption. Encourage the woman by reserving your attention for her until her turn is over. If you don't catch on to the fact that a man has usurped the floor until after the fact, you can still say, "I didn't get all of what Amy said because Bill interrupted her. Amy, will you repeat what you were saying a while ago about the Literature Department?"

Sometimes we try to protect ourselves against interruption by filling our speech with pads. "Mmmmmmmm, hm, let me see, aaaaaaah" is one way to signal that you haven't finished your thoughts. It is more effective, however, to hang on to your speaking turn by maintaining eye contact and falling silent. If someone tries to interrupt while you collect your thoughts, look at him squarely and lift one hand in a gentle gesture to indicate that you do not wish to relinquish the floor. When you allow your eyes to drop to your lap someone will inevitably try to interrupt even if you make "stalling" sounds.

Encourage women to talk. "Hold it a sec, Bill, I believe I saw Amy shake her head. Amy, did you have a comment?"

The chair can say, "I'm sure we would like to hear all your ideas, Bernard; however, I want to get full participation from everyone. Please hold on until the others have had a chance to comment."

If a woman offers a point and the next speaker takes off in a different direction say, "Is this where we want to be going? We seem to have digressed from Amy's point." Or, "Ralph, I suggest we take that up as soon as we finish the subject at hand, which is Amy's suggestion that..."

Provide one another with opportunities to speak. "Cindy, you've had more experience with this than most of us. Do you have any suggestions?"

Congratulate, thank and praise one another on good points.

If a man seems to be running off with the credit for an idea originally posed by a woman, point it out. "I don't think we could correctly term that 'Bill's resolution' since it is an elaboration of what Amy said an hour ago." Or, "Bill, I like your modification of Amy's suggestion." Don't let a man take credit for your contributions, either. Jump right in with "Oh, I'm glad you all have picked up on my suggestion. I was afraid at last week's meeting that you hadn't heard me."

A woman will often allow a man to present her ideas. Take credit for what you do by presenting your own results in meetings; do not let your male boss or male coworker do it for you.

Confront what is really going on. If you can see that all the women have lowered their eyes, folded their arms and started to withdraw, say, "I'm beginning to get the feeling that several of us (a) disagree with what is going on, (b) feel Sharon's suggestion was dismissed too quickly, (c) are getting angry."

Look at the woman who is talking. Your eye contact and responsiveness will make her feel supported.

Notice how men and women take up space. Power is often visible in the expansive relaxed obtrusive posture of the in group and the constricted, circumspect, condensed posture of the out group. Check yourself for defensive posture; rigidly clasped arms, for instance. Does your face feel pinched and drawn? If you modify your tight body language perhaps your feelings will change.

If you have to go through your papers or your pocketbook or go to the restroom or speak to the person next to you, don't do it while another woman is talking.

Sometimes we hate the combat and competition that goes on when men are present so much that we don't want ever to have to prove anything or argue for anything again. We find these discouraged feelings are relieved, though, when we feel the support of other women.

A Word about Workshops and Panels

If you have thirty participants in your workshop, you may subdivide into five groups of six people each to engage in a task, solve a problem or do an exercise. The chair makes opening remarks, gives information or instruction, and wraps-up, but her main job is to assist participants in doing their own learning or experiencing.

A panel is usually made up of three or four speakers and a

moderator. The purpose is to provide the audience with several opinions or perspectives on a single topic. A panel can be made up of speakers who have different kinds of expertise in a general area; it is a good idea to form them with people of different ages and races. Panelists may agree or disagree with one another; all they need to have in common is the topic and coordination by the moderator.

A good moderator will talk to all the panelists before the day of the presentation to elicit enough information to introduce each of them well and to be certain that they are all aware of what the others plan to say so there will be no duplication of speeches. She stipulates the time limit for their presentations. (Allow at least one-third of the time for questions and answers.)

A moderator does not deliver a speech herself. It is her job to maintain a firm hand and benign air, to make sure each panelist observes her time limit, and to interrupt a speaker who is taking more than a fair share of the time. The moderator introduces each speaker and refers to her by name often (huge placecards on the table in front of the speaker are recommended). The moderator makes transitional remarks in between speakers. (For example, "Dr. Dingbat certainly makes some interesting points about the value of professional training." "Ms. Ardent, will you tell us your views on the philosophy of a feminist self-help clinic?") After the last speaker has finished, the moderator sums up briefly and opens the panel to questions from the audience. If there are no questions, the moderator asks one herself. The moderator prods, coaxes (and plants) good questions—she also tries to clarify (or paraphrase) ambiguous questions or answers. In some cases, time may be allotted for the speakers on the panel to question one another or respond to other speakers' statements. It is the moderator's job to call on questioners and to direct their questions to panel members—this is to prevent one panelist from monopolizing the question and answer period.

Panels are usually fun for speakers and audience alike because of the variety of opinions and because there is time for informal exchange among panelists and audience. As a panelist you can think of it as a bridge game—you must play not only your own hand but also your partner's. It is a team speech, so you need to know what the others plan to talk about. A panel is a cooperative venture even when the speakers disagree, and it can be exhilarating to reason, discuss and differ together.

CHAPTER ELEVEN

Media

Only ten years ago it would have been preposterous to include a chapter on media—especially radio and TV—in a book for women. The information would have been relevant to few. Today, however, nearly every woman who reads *Speaking Up* will have the opportunity to "do" media at some time or another. The proliferation of talk shows, the emphasis on feminist programming, the large numbers of women entering work roles requiring public presentations for their organizations, and finally the legitimation we women are giving one another's desire to be heard all make it likely that tips on radio and TV will be useful to the woman who is not a professional public speaker.

The Telephone

Think of each phone call as a speech, that is, a form of self-presentation for which you have objectives, must organize your ideas and communicate them well. You have an audience for a phone call; you can connect with that audience well or poorly. Too often we pick up the phone impulsively and begin the dialogue before we have planned what we want to say or how we want to say it. Hence, we have conversations that drag on interminably in which we fail to persuade, do not get what we want and do not say what we meant to say. A too-hasty call to a prospective employer or a relative can result in shambles.

Effective communication does not mean making great speeches. It means great habits. Treat a phone call as seriously as you would a face-to-face conversation or personal interview.

Consider, as you would in an impromptu speech, what you want the point or conclusion of the conversation to be. Prepare opening "lines" to broach difficult topics.

Make notes so you won't have to phone back over and over with details you forgot to mention in the first call. We also suggest you make notes while you are conversing. If you jot down a point you want to raise, you can return to active listening and not interrupt the person who is talking. It is difficult to concentrate on what someone is saying if you are simultaneously trying to hold your own point in mind for the next pause.

Begin conversations by clearing the time: "This isn't a good time for me to talk. May I return your call at 3:00?" "I'd like to talk to you for about ten minutes. Is this a good time for you?" "I can only talk for a few minutes and then I have to write my column."

It may be an astonishingly useful and revealing exercise to tape record your side of a phone conversation. Listen critically to the tape for voice quality, passive or aggressive approaches to discussion, fillers and detractors.

On the telephone, just as on radio, your warmth, sincerity and your mood must be expressed by your voice alone because the listener cannot see you. Body language, facial animation and physical appearance don't count. Attach stickers to your phones for visual reminders to keep your pitch low, your volume adequate and your "ums" to a minimum.

Many individuals and businesses now use telephone answering devices. If you fail to leave a message, the machine will blast thirty seconds of dial tone at the person you called. A message (your name, the time you called, and your phone number) is much nicer to hear on playback.

Radio and TV

> Nothing in life is to be feared.
> It is only to be understood.
> MARIE CURIE

If you have never had a chance to be in the studio audience for a talk show or witness a radio broadcast, we encourage you to do so as soon as it is practical. The scariness will evaporate with the mystery once you experience being inside a studio, seeing the sets and learning how things work.

Most local TV talk show producers have trouble filling their studios with audiences day in and day out; sometimes station employees are dragged away from their desks to sit in for an hour to swell the crowd. Some stations have to award prizes or gifts to entice people. If you have never been inside a television station, why not pick up the phone right away and find out which programs welcome live audiences, when they tape, and what time you have to arrive. College radio stations are often casual about studio visitors; it is better if you know someone who can escort you around, but even if you don't you will probably be able to sit in on a show.

Television stations offer air time to the community for Public Service Announcements. Call or write your local station to ask for information on PSA's. After you have read the rules, you will probably realize that several issues you care a lot about would be appropriate topics for PSA's. You may belong to some interest group that wants to communicate a message; a PSA is a good way to speak out. You can write and submit a PSA either as an individual or as an authorized representative of a group.

Station technicians realize that almost everyone who tapes a PSA is going on the air for the first time. They usually allow a few minutes for you to rehearse once or twice before taping. A Public Service Announcement taping is great practice in establishing eye contact with a camera and using a TelePrompTer.

When You Are the Guest. Don't be surprised to discover that the cordial and sympathetic moderator who chats with you before you go on the air becomes the "role incumbent" as soon as the red lights flash. Her job is to get an exciting and entertaining interview. Just because the host meets you and "warms you up" doesn't mean that she will gently skirt subject areas you don't want to discuss, or will try to avoid upsetting you or will have the common decency not to ask embarrassing personal questions on the air. A moderator tries to be calm and friendly with guests before going on the air because a terrified guest is a stiff one. Once you are at ease, the gentle host begins to do her job—and she may see her job as putting you on the spot. To her, your comfort may be secondary to a memorable interview.

"Off the record" conversations or requests to stay away from certain subjects will do absolutely no good if the show starts to drag. The host's priority is vitality, and she or he will sensationalize a segment if necessary.

The best way to avoid trouble in a radio or TV interview is to give them what they want in the first place. Present your interviewer-to-be and the show's producer with a list of hard-hitting, fascinating questions before air time. You don't have to be at cross-purposes with them; your best interests are served when the conversation is lively, too. Prepare answers that supply drama or controversy so the host won't have to go poking for it.

We also suggest that you send the moderator basic information about your topic. Make the info sheets concise; most talk show hosts don't read an author's book, for instance, before interviewing the author.

Radio and TV programming is aimed to appeal to the broadest possible market; producers assume low intelligence and/or total ignorance on the part of listeners and viewers.

Be prepared to give basic definitions of your terms and a general explanation of your topic because the producer's premise is that the audience has zero information. Remember, too, that anecdotes and examples work better than abstract explanations; they are more fun.

An actress is used to getting up in front of an audience night after night and saying the same lines with all the emotion she can. It is harder for the rest of us to repeat ourselves because we want to appear unstudied, unrehearsed and natural. Most of us are self-conscious and embarrassed if we have to repeat a story in front of someone who has already heard us tell it, and often instead of repeating the story the best way, we try to change it so it will seem original or spontaneous to the listener who has heard it before. The host, producer and other station employees who talk to you before the show want to hear what you will say on the air. Later, try to forget they've heard it before. Say what you came to say uninhibited by the fact that you are repeating yourself.

Taped programs are usually edited only if the guest says something obscene or libelous. Your show will be aired with whatever mistakes, pauses or fumblings you make. The only difference between a taped show and a live show is the broadcast date.

Radio

A radio appearance is the least threatening way to break into speaking. No one can see you. You don't have to worry about eye contact or appearing nervous. Your movements don't have to be controlled and your hair doesn't have to be combed.

Yet, like any other speech situation, preparation and practice are important. Spontaneity and planning are mutually reinforcing, not mutually exclusive. The best radio guests bring a list or an outline with them so they are sure to get in what they want to say.

Your Homework. Find out ahead of time exactly what is going to happen. How long will the interview last? Will there be phone calls, music breaks or commercials to interrupt your interview?

Tell your friends and relatives you are going to be on the radio. If the show is a call-in, plant a lot of calls and questions with friends. Ask them to write the station after the show to thank the producers for bringing such an interesting topic and guest to the air, and to request more programming on your topic.

At the Studio. An engineer will do a sound check before you tape/go on the air. If you pop your *P*'s or hiss your *S*'s, you may be asked to speak across your mike rather than directly into it. This means that the mike will be turned, or that your chair will be placed at a new angle. When it is time for the voice check, turn to the moderator and begin to tell her your name and address and the subjects for tonight's show just as though you are on the air. It drives engineers crazy when a guest can't think of anything to say for the voice check, or recites the alphabet in a mousy, hesitant way then proceeds to use an entirely different volume level when she actually speaks on the air. When you are miked for a speech before an audience you stand back far enough (and/or have the sound level adjusted) so that you still have to project your voice. So, too, in radio the ideal is to speak in normal tones, not soft ones. Low volume communicates low energy. Fortunately for us, microphones usually transmit female voices more clearly and warmly than male voices, regardless of the actual distance of the speaker from the mike.

Many radio producers ask guests to wear headsets, especially if there are several guests on the air at the same time. Headphones are a bit uncomfortable, and make you look funny, but they can mean the difference between a good presentation and a poor one. The reason is simple. Headphones let you hear what the audience hears; you can tell instantly when you are not speaking directly into the mike, making too much noise flipping through your notes or tapping the mike stand with your pencil. If you hear yourself sounding weak and faraway, it is probably because you have turned your head too far to one side to look at the guest sitting next to you. Eye contact stimulates energy, because the response from another person turns us on; yet if you go "off mike," all is lost.

During the Program. Heed the warnings station employees give you about their equipment. Some equipment is old and unsophisticated and you won't be able to move around much without going out of microphone range. If you bump or tap the mike it will probably broadcast thunderously.

We suggest you keep your mouth approximately three inches from the mike. Lean forward in your chair because this will make you feel (and therefore sound) more animated. Do not pick up the mike or move it. We suggest that you use note *cards;* they don't rustle as paper does. Don't wear clanky jewelry and, finally, don't drink carbonated beverages before or during the show.

The host and the engineer will use hand signals to communicate with each other when you are on the air. We have included a chart of a few common moderator's signals for you. Try not to be distracted by these gestures. The moderator will explain any signals that are meant for you (for example, a "wrap it up, we're running out of time" signal). Ignore the rest.

Bear in mind that people can't absorb as much information when they are listening as they can when they are reading or watching TV. If you talk about something complex or if you use numbers it is very important to paraphrase, to give clear examples and to repeat. Repeat key phrases for those who just got into the car and turned on the radio.

Unlike members of a live audience, listeners in a radio audience are likely to tune into the program in the middle. The audience has no faces to associate with and is likely to forget who you are, even if the moderator gave you an excellent introduction. Write the name of the host and anyone else on the air with you on a cue card and use their names frequently in the conversation. On TV, the guests' names are flashed on the bottom of the screen from time to time, but it is still nice to call the others by name.

Radio flattens a speaker out. Make a special effort to be exciting, dramatic and colorful. If you are a slow speaker, put "speed up" reminders in front of you. (Fast talkers sound better on the radio than they do in "real life.") When an audience can see you they are patient when they have to wait while you fumble for a word or think of a response to a question. On the radio this is called "dead air" and it is what every announcer dreads. Listeners who are fiddling with the dial will pass right over a silent station.

A good radio announcer (and guest) presents everything as though it just occurred to her for the first time at that very moment. The excitement in your voice depends in part on how involved you can be with the person you are talking to. Lean forward and talk *to* the host. Unfortunately, the host will have to disengage from time to time, look away from you to signal the engineer, consult her notes while you talk, watch the buttons on her phone setup etcetera. It isn't easy to converse like this, but just keep rolling as though you had her undivided attention. Rivet your face to hers for those moments when she *is* able to reestablish eye contact; if you talk to your lap your voice will die.

Call-in Shows. If the program is the call-in type, expect a great many calls from older listeners. A large proportion of radio audiences consists of shut-ins.

It is especially important to remember that almost all of the calls you will receive will be from individuals who want to disagree with your point of view and/or who tuned in late, misunderstood your point of view and want to disagree or ask irrelevant questions. The people who are motivated to call are usually the ones who are angry with you. This is a built-in fact of radio life and not a reflection on you. Be gracious. Get to the emotional biases that prompt the hostile questions in the first place. Do not argue. Stick to the points

Standby: A warning signal to tell the engineer that you want her to be ready to do something in fifteen seconds or so.

Start it or do it: Tells the engineer to do whatever it is she is supposed to do next. Usually it means to start a record or tape or cartridge. You should spell out what you expect in advance.

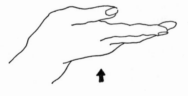

Fade-up: Increase the level of volume of whatever's on the air. In the case of a "talk-over" this means increase the music level.

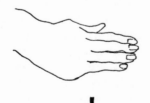

Fade down: Decrease the level of whatever's on the air.

Microphone on the air: This tells the engineer to put your mike on.

Cut the mike: Takes you off the air.

Station break: A pause in the program to give the station I.D. which consists of the call letters and the city in which the station is located. I.D.'s should be given as close to the hour as possible, every hour, at a natural break in the program.

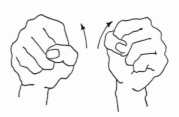

Roll theme: Tells the engineer to start your theme music. In cases when you are "backtiming" your show to end at the logged time exactly, the theme should be started, but not faded up until the rest of the program has ended.

you came to express and don't let yourself get sidetracked.

Do not allow yourself to sound exasperated or arrogant. It is the show host's job to cut people off, not yours.

Be brief if calls are coming in thick and fast. If the switchboard isn't lighting up, be prepared to keep talking; your list of subsidiary points and issues will help. Remember that this radio conversation is just like any other speech—if you aren't getting the response you want, your natural tendency may be to get safer, smaller and duller, to pretend you aren't there or that you don't care. Go to the other extreme, behave as though everything were just fine. And remember, the worst thing that can happen on radio is dead air.

Television

> If I could I would always work in silence and obscurity, and let my efforts be known by their results.
>
> EMILY BRONTË

"Talk" has become a spectator sport. If you have success at anything from bank robbery to bird-watching, sooner or later you will be invited to converse for the benefit of an eavesdropping public.

Before the Show. Wear something that is easy to *sit* in. Avoid white, small busy prints, flashy jewelry that may catch the lights, or any jewelry that makes noise when you move. If you wear slacks, make certain they don't ride halfway up your calf when you're seated. If you wear a dress or a skirt, pay special attention to length. You don't want to have to tug your hemline down over your thighs on the air.

TV lights are hot. Consider wearing dress shields. You may want to take a sweater to the studio, which is air conditioned, to wear just until you step up on the set, where the lights will be uncomfortably warm.

Comb your hair in back. Camera angles are unkind to those

who are only groomed in the front. If you can, watch the show a few times before your appearance on it to see what kind of posture seems to work best for the guests who occupy the chair you will shortly occupy. On the "Today" program, for example, most guests are shown in more extreme profile than the host(s). The faces of guests with long hair are often obscured because there are no frontal camera shots.

Do not touch the equipment. Since lavaliere and clip-on microphones must be fastened to your clothes by union members you will have to endure the (usually male) technician who reaches inside your collar.

On the Air. Most TV talk show segments run between five and eight minutes. Better enjoy the attention, because it will be over in a hurry.

As a guest on a talk show you can be conversational, informal and colloquial. Your eye contact with the interviewer should be steady and sustained. This is one time you do *not* want to make eye contact with everyone in the room. If you look out into the studio audience, or at the technicans and camera crew to try to include them in what you are saying, the impression on the viewers at home will be that your eyes are wandering all over the place. The viewers cannot see who it is you are trying to include.

The exception is when a speech you are making is being filmed or videotaped. In this case, look directly into the camera, just as though the camera were another person in the audience. The result is that the people who view the film later will feel included as audience members.

The camera with the red light on is the one in use. There are two, sometimes three, cameras for a talk show, and the one in use will keep changing. Ignore the camera. Just talk to the moderator.

Keep your hands away from your face and avoid jerky movements. Don't whip your head around from host to fellow guest and back. Leisurely movements are best, such as when you change position in your chair.

TV combines long shots with close-ups. The movement of

the eyelid or eyebrow, or the quiver of the lip that might be perfectly eloquent will be lost on a long shot, while a gross movement of the arm will be lost in a close-up where only the miniature movements can be seen. The only solution is to be yourself and hope the odds are with you; some of your facial animation will be captured and so will some of your deadpan or severe expressions.

It is true that TV will make you appear about ten pounds heavier. And a camera operator who wants to can make you look absolutely terrible. It is small comfort, we know, but it isn't always our fault when we seem fat, slow and under-educated.

Meet the Press

> I don't care what you write as long as you spell my name right.
> AMERICAN CLICHÉ

The saying "I don't care what they say about me as long as they're talking about me" had better have some validity for your situation before you take your case to the public. The chances of accurate reporting of your views, issue or event are slim, so the first consideration is whether it's worth it to get media attention at all.

By all means, tape your remarks in a press interview or at a press conference and certainly have copies of the text of any statement you make. But don't count on a correction, a retraction or an apology if you are misquoted.

Reporters are people. Each reporter brings to a news event limited information, exposure, intelligence, analytical ability and time. Each reporter has different ideas about what is newsworthy. Each reporter has an interest in writing good copy, and sometimes that interest conflicts with what she perceives as the dull news you have to offer. Each reporter has limitations of space, and often must oversimplify or omit the full context for facts or statements you provide. This may mean that your news is distorted or falsified. As this book goes to press, the emphasis in the media on personality talk and gossip is stronger than ever and "hard" news is suffering.

Readers are no more discriminating than reporters; it is amazing how often an article that you perceive as "damaging" to you turns out not to be. Ask which risk is greater: to have readers know something incorrect or to know nothing at all.

The Women's Action Alliance has published a very good booklet about how to plan a press conference. (For ordering information see Catherine Samuels in the bibliography.) Here are a few of our suggestions for "handling" the press.

If you are a participant in a press conference, you and the other speakers will each deliver a brief prepared statement. Rehearse your statement thoroughly so that you can say it to the camera/audience, only checking with your notes from time to time. By all means, look alive while the others are talking and do not do anything to call attention to yourself when it is someone else's turn to speak.

News producers often decide what to broadcast on the basis of what they have the videotape to support, not on the basis of what is most important for the audience to know. Plan some movement such as a presentation, a signing ceremony or perhaps demonstrate something or display something. You are more likely to appear on TV or be photographed if your news involves something visual. It helps if the setting for the press conference is visually interesting. Pay attention to the backdrop. Try to seat all the speakers close enough together so that TV crews will have no trouble filming everything from the same spot in the room. If they have to move the camera equipment around they may disturb print media reporters who are trying to take notes.

The TV crew may ask you to repeat your statement or the presentation of the award several times until they have it on tape the way they want it.

You have very little time in a press conference. Reporters are always in a hurry. Begin on time and don't waste time answering irrelevant questions. Expect antagonism if the press is hostile to you or to your issue. Reporters want you to make colorful statements and they may try to get you riled up to get them. Don't allow anyone or anything to take you off your points. "That is an interesting point/question, but even more fascinating is...."; "I'd love to answer that for you later. Right now I think most people are wondering..." Irrelevant questions absorb precious minutes you need to deliver your message. Yes, be quotable, but not on extraneous matters.

It helps to be nice to reporters. Feature writers get to say what kind of impression you made and pass along value judgments on you. If you are charming, warm and funny they may say so. If you are cranky they may say that, too. But acting nice and devoting all the time the reporter requests to provide information and background will not guarantee accuracy. We might as well accept the fact that reporters are interested in what sells papers. Complex and difficult analysis does not sell papers. Media will print/air what is accessible. Yes, try to provide the background, the context, the facts that make what you say comprehensible. Yes, be courteous and yes, dodge irrelevant questions. But give short answers when you can and expect out-of-context quotes when you can't. Use examples to support your generalizations. And finally, don't become so excited you say something you want to take back later. Whenever you are interviewed at a press conference or for an on-the-spot news item, do your best to keep your pitch down, speak deliberately and avoid wild exaggeration. ("The filthy capitalist supermarket owners will be brought to their knees by our boycott. We won't stand for it and neither of us is afraid to say so!") Bear in mind that your statements may sound completely hysterical in contrast to the custard-smooth reporters.

A FINAL WORD

If, after having carefully read and taken to heart every word in this book, you still feel inadequate, inarticulate and unequal to the task, here's our advice: do it anyway. Nobody ever feels completely comfortable speaking in public and at some point one simply has to throw oneself into the lake and hope one can swim.

The dominants keep themselves dominant by making a lot of rules about How Things Are Done. In effect, this means that they can always say, "Well, I suppose you *have* learned to fix a car, earn money, run a business or a country, but you don't do it RIGHT." Then they chuckle about hairpins and ruffles in the board room and try to make you miss the point, which is to do it, to get the job done.

You don't need to mimic any particular style or adopt anybody else's stupid rules. And you don't have to be perfect to have a right to be heard. You just have to close your eyes and jump.

We would a thousand times rather see women standing up boring everyone to death, going blank, screeching, giggling and making no sense at all than sitting in the back of the room keeping their mouths shut because they are too "polite" to impose themselves on others. We've all done that and know it is a hype. Speaking up is better.

BIBLIOGRAPHY

ALLEN, PAMELA: *Free Space: A Perspective on the Small Group in Women's Liberation,* Times Change Press, New York, 1970.

BARTLETT, JOHN: *Bartlett's Familiar Quotations,* Little, Brown & Co., Boston, 1968.

BLOOM, LYNN Z., KAREN COBURN AND JOAN PEARLMAN: *The New Assertive Woman,* Dell Publishing Co., Inc., 1975.
How to know what you feel, say what you mean and get what you want.

DREIFUS, CLAUDIA: *Woman's Fate,* Bantam Books, Inc., New York, 1973.
Raps from a feminist consciousness-raising group.

FLEXNER, ELEANOR: *Century of Struggle: The Woman's Rights Movement in the United States,* Atheneum, New York, 1968.
Basic history of the first wave of feminism in the United States.

FOLLETT, WILSON: *Modern American Usage,* Warner Paperback, New York, 1974.
Why Grand Central isn't a station and other fascinating pedantry.

GARSON, BARBARA: *All the Livelong Day: The Meaning and De-*

meaning of Routine Work, Doubleday and Company, Inc., New York, p. xiii, 1975.

HENLEY, NANCY: *Body Politics*, Prentice-Hall, New Jersey, 1977. Highly recommended. Excellent reading about power, sex and nonverbal communication.

LAKOFF, ROBIN: *Language and Woman's Place*, Harper Colophon Books, New York, 1975.

LASH, JOSEPH P.: *Eleanor and Franklin*, Signet, New York, 1973. Includes how Eleanor Roosevelt learned to speak in public.

MARTIN, DEL: *The Battered Wives of America*, Glide Publications, 330 Ellis St., San Francisco, California 94102, 1975.

McGraw-Hill Book Company, *Guidelines for Equal Treatment of the Sexes.*
To obtain a free copy, send your name and address to McGraw-Hill, 1221 Avenue of the Americas, New York, New York 10020.

MILLER, CASEY, AND KATE SWIFT: *Words and Women*, Doubleday (Anchor Press), New York, New York, 1976.
Why *Modern American Usage* is often wrong even though "correct."

OAKLEY, MARY ANN B.: *Elizabeth Cady Stanton*, The Feminist Press, Old Westbury, New York, 1972.
How women first got up the nerve to speak for themselves, among other things. Write to The Feminist Press, Box 334, Old Westbury, New York 11568 for a catalogue.

ROBERT, HENRY: *Robert's Rules of Order*, William Morrow, New York, 1971.

ROGET, PETER MARK: *New Roget's Thesaurus in Dictionary Form*, Berkeley Publishing Co., New York, New York, 1969.

SAMUELS, CATHERINE: *How to Make the Media Work for You*, Woman's Action Alliance, New York, New York, 1975.
To order, send your name and address and a check for $3 to Women's Action Alliance, 370 Lexington Avenue, New York, New York 10017.

SARNOFF, DOROTHY: *Speech Can Change Your Life*, Dell Publishing Company, Inc., New York, 1972.

STRUNK, WILLIAM, AND E. B. WHITE: *Elements of Style*, Macmillan, New York, 1972.

THORNE, BARRIE, AND NANCY HENLEY: *Language and Sex*, Newbury House, Rowley, Massachusetts, 1975.

Includes an annotated bibliography of sex difference in language, speech and nonverbal communication. Send your name, address and a check for $8.95 to Newbury House, 54 Warehouse Lane, Rowley, Massachusetts 01969.